THE INVITATION

Rich and Raw Conversations
about Aging, Death and Dying

To Rita,
Thanks for your support and love!
Ruth Tamari

THE INVITATION

Rich and Raw Conversations
about Aging, Death and Dying

RUTH TAMARI, MEd., CPCC

Copyright © 2017 by Ruth Tamari

All rights reserved.

Cover illustration by Caroline Kubela
Book cover design by Allyson Woodrooffe
Text design by Kathleen Doody

www.ruthtamari.com

No part of this book may be reproduced in any form or by any electronic or mechanical means including information storage and retrieval systems, without permission in writing from the author, except in the case of brief quotations embodied in critical articles and reviews.

The names may have been changed to protect the privacy of those mentioned in this publication.

ISBN 978-0-9959767-0-2

Table of Contents

1	Ruth's Thoughts on Aging and How The Interview Project Began	1
2	Emily	17
3	Brad	25
4	Mariana	33
5	Joel	39
6	Gabriele	49
7	Lucy	57
8	Ruth's Thoughts on Dying: How I Became An Amazonian	63
9	David	77
10	Courtney	85
11	Sylvia	93
12	Joanne	103
13	Jane	113
14	Ruth's Thoughts on Death: What I Missed	121
15	Doug	129
16	Rose	137
17	Varda	145
18	Maggie	157
19	Edna	167
20	The Story About John or I Killed a Man	177
21	Your Invitation: The Questions Your Notes	181 / 185
22	Acknowledgments	189

*Dedicated with love to
Rachel and George Tamari*

1

Ruth's Thoughts on Aging

My first memory of old people is when I was five years old, nestled among my grandparents, great-aunt and great-uncle. Of course, I didn't understand what old meant then. My mom and I were visiting relatives in Israel, three years after our family immigrated to Canada. They were in their 60s and 70s. They had wrinkles and grey hair, wore plain clothes, and wore ugly eyeglasses for reading and sewing. My grandparents and I did not speak the same language — I spoke English and a rudimentary Hebrew; they spoke Hungarian and a rudimentary Hebrew — so words were not what connected us.

One particular sweltering Jerusalem afternoon we were resting in my great-aunt and great-uncle's small living room. My mom sat on the enormous rose sofa bed, her feet not quite reaching the floor, while I lay nestled in the fold of her lap. My grandmother, grandfather, great-aunt and great-uncle sat across from us in armchairs, forming a circle. They sliced and cored succulent, room-temperature fruit: peaches, apples, apricots, and plums. Hands peeled an apple with quiet experience and knowing — how much pressure, how to slice both thinly and thickly enough. The sweet aromas of the fruit blended with their soft voices. As small as the room was, it felt spacious: the humid air was filled with gentleness, hushed grace and consideration. I noticed how little they had and that they were ready to share all of it, give it away too. In this nest of grand-elders I felt protected, cherished and nourished in every way.

They patiently taught me card games, folk songs, and homemade recipes. They played, joked, sang, and laughed with me, Granddad stirring the "chicken soup" as the ice cream melted in the bowl. They embraced me all the time in their soft, strong arms and showered me with kisses. The powerful feelings of belonging and connection washed through and over me. I felt totally adored by them and my love for them was locked in. My shyness disappeared that summer and my confidence blossomed — I bloomed into a talkative, outgoing little girl.

Like many immigrant families, we were only able to visit every few years. The next time was when I was an 11-year-old preteen. And then when I was a very adolescent 16-year-old, my parents and I visited for my maternal grandmother's unveiling, and because my dad's mother, Regina, was very ill.

Regina had the bluest eyes and wore cat-eye glasses. She was thin from ulcerative issues caused by Holocaust trauma. Her stomach never recovered. It worsened so that she was bone thin. She moved into a nursing home after becoming very frail. The only pleasures she still enjoyed were sweets and the occasional cigarette. My mom and I brought her a Danish, cut it up into bite-sized pieces, and she asked me to feed them to her. Regina and I watched each other's blue eyes. Few words were exchanged during this intimate moment. Afterwards, with her elegant, long, bony fingers she held up a cigarette to be lit and then inhaled deeply, curls of smoke billowing up around her. She died six weeks later and, I hope, at peace.

These tender moments with my elders remain with me. Little did I know that they gifted me with something invaluable: accepting and loving my aging self. I saw how they looked with their wrinkles, their grey hair, their soft skin, and what I would look like when I would live as many years as they had. I also saw how I would be: confident, kind and full of love. They were role models of the elder I wanted to become.

It was only decades later that I understood that it was even more amazing that their humour, caring and love had survived hardship, tragedy and trauma. They had lived through divorce, addiction, mental illness, war and genocide. Their children were killed; their relatives were killed. They had gone through immigration and resettlement. Their hearts broke; their hearts healed and connected anew. They lived well into their 70s, 80s, even past 100. Their strength after facing numerous life challenges was a present to me — they modelled how to be resilient. I have learned that I can handle anything because they could and did.

When each of them died, they were abroad and felt so far away. I wonder what it was they were experiencing, thinking, feeling, wanting. I will never know and that saddens me. I suppose it is the universal longing of immigrant families and grandchildren who are separated by distance from their grandparents.

This special connection with my grand-elders echoed with other seniors. In university, while studying psychology, sociology and gerontology, I chose to do practicum fieldwork in long-term care residences, including a hospital continuing-care unit. I felt "at home" and met others who felt likewise. I had no idea this was an anomaly, not shared by most people. By age 23, I had found my calling and started a career in geriatric health care, a most honourable but unsexy choice. I was hired at Baycrest Centre for Geriatric Care as a recreation therapist. Baycrest is a Jewish healthcare organization that serves a wide continuum of older adults over 60, from those who are healthy and live independently in the community to people who have multiple illnesses and are frail. For 20 years, I worked at Baycrest in both community and long-term care settings: the Day Treatment Centre, the Jewish Home for the Aged, the Community Recreation Outreach Program, the Complex Continuing Care and Inpatient Psychiatry units in the hospital, and the Mood Disorders Clinic.

During the daytime, the main floor was filled with seniors. They were in the Centre or down from their rooms — to visit someone, to volunteer, on their way to a program or a clinic appointment, maybe to have a change of scenery. Some walked independently, some were escorted in reclining wheelchairs with IV bags attached, others used two-wheeled walkers or brightly coloured Rollators in burgundy, teal and purple with their enviable pullout seats, and a few people had gastronomy tubes attached to their abdomen for feeding nourishment to stay alive.

In Judaism it is considered a "mitzvah," a good deed, to show care and respect for one's elders. Elders were addressed as Mister or Missus, unless they had explicitly requested to be called by their first name or nickname. Porters escorted clients from their hospital or nursing room to clinic appointments. Staff or volunteers accompanied clients to programs.

Everyone was valued for their abilities and the space was accessible to all. Every effort was made by medical teams to ensure that individuals participated in their programs of interest. The weekly team rounds discussed how to provide the best quality of life. The creative arts studio was open to senior residents of every artistic ability. Mature volunteers worked as cashiers at the café, as meal-feeding support for people who had difficulty swallowing, and as program assistants who offered much-needed connection to those who were very ill.

During mid-afternoon coffee breaks, I loved to go down to the cafeteria for the rugelach, small cinnamon or chocolate crescent rolls. In the lobby, I schmoozed with clients, companions, volunteers, colleagues and staff. Those moments of connection with elders and this community restored and nourished me, as much as the delicious rugelach. It was a rich education to experience in my 20s.

After a few years I went off to complete a master's degree in counselling psychology and adult education. When I returned I was assigned to a "Special Care" floor in the nursing home. It was a locked unit for people who had moderate to late-stage illnesses including Parkinson's disease, stroke, Alzheimer's, frontal lobe dementia, among others. Arriving onto the floor and stepping out of the elevator was a sensory overload. A row of residents was gathered around in wheelchairs and armchairs, tucked against the walls, greeting me with smiles, stares, and the occasional drool. Smells of soiled hampers and puréed food hung in the air. Greetings of hello mingled with cries of pain and involuntary vocalizations. It felt institutional, overwhelming and sad — sad with the smell of patient waiting and loneliness. It was disappointing to discover how few people received regular visits from their family members.

Incredible that twelve months earlier I had worked here, at the Centre, and had become desensitized to the environment. What had been familiar was now foreign to me. It was strange for a while, until these strangers and I became familiar. Until we knew each other's name, voice, likes, dislikes and moods. Until my new colleagues and I became friends. Until I knew the spaces for what they were meant to do, and where everything was stored and waiting for me to share. Until I became part of this community. I worked as a front-line clinician in the nursing home for two years, and then transferred to work with clients in the community. The lonely sadness that lived in long-term care overwhelmed me and I felt ineffective at improving it. My respect and admiration deepened for colleagues who were able to create an inspiring environment and caring community over the long term.

One thing happened over and over again. No matter where I worked in the Centre, family members said to me, "Wow, I could never do what you're doing." These words stunned me. They were sons and daughters, nieces and nephews, siblings and cousins. They were professional men and women, many in their mid-life years. I shared this with my colleagues who had also heard the same sentiment. I wondered to myself, "Why could you never do this? Why could you never take loving care of elders?"

It all changed the moment I realized my dad had a serious memory loss. I remember it was a Friday. I don't remember what exactly happened that led to my realization, but I can picture myself at home, sobbing. I stayed close to bed that entire weekend, looking up at the high stuccoed ceiling as streams of tears and snot poured from me. The taupe walls held me tight as I wept for him, and for me. I remember looking outside from my bed and seeing the enormous old oak trees, the skies peeking through the branches. I don't remember the time of year, just the shocking moment when this was etched into my being.

As a geriatric clinician, I understood the prognosis and what to expect. I knew the journey that we were supposed to go on — my dad, my mom and me, as their only family member living nearby. There were many things that we were supposed to do. We were supposed to help him live for as long as possible in spite of his loss of independence, competence, identity and dignity. We were supposed to admit him into a long-term care facility if his cognitive losses and health issues became unmanageable at home.

Except, I did not want that to happen. As scared as I was to have to go into this frightening unknown, I did know many things: about myself, about my dad's wishes, about how to care and respect elders, about health care, and about treatment decisions. I felt anxious but I also felt prepared. I was going to need all of that for what I was about to experience.

My dad did not say much about dying or death, but thankfully my mom did. She talked about it and planned it for as long as I can remember. She studied comparative religions for years and was a member of the organization, Dying With Dignity, from its very beginning. She talked about her funeral, the music she wanted played and the poems she wanted read. She talked about advanced directives and powers of attorney and living wills and finances and estate planning and assisted dying. She spoke about it all the time to the point that we joked about it, "Okay, here it comes. Can I get a cup of tea first?" I could almost recite to her all the things she wanted for her dying and death. In the meantime, she had made talking about it feel natural, honest, humourous and loving. My dad seemed to agree — philosophically and spiritually — and if he felt differently, I'm sure he would have expressed it quite eloquently. He never mentioned his funeral or planned the details of his celebration of life; maybe he wanted the family to make it however we needed it to be.

As I turned 40, I experienced career dissatisfaction working in the medicalized health care system along with the typical mid-life angst, questioning, "What's next?" and "What will grow and challenge me?" After exploring for a while, I discovered life coaching and thought it might be a profession where I could help address, even prevent, issues I had witnessed. I wanted to focus on aging and life transitions from a holistic perspective and with adults of all ages, not only those who were over 60.

I slowly moved into this new career, and a new identity of entrepreneur. As I worked to establish myself, business coaches, image consultants and marketing experts asked me about the impression I wanted to make. There were implicit suggestions about how I should present myself: youthful, attractive, vibrant, energetic, with a dose of "wow" factor to get new clients and help me become a successful entrepreneur.

Only after I began to pursue my new coaching career out in the "real world" did I realize how unique the geriatric care environment was. That community really cared about older adults and people were respected for their age and experience, wrinkles and all. I had been enclosed in that warm bubble and it burst. I walked face-first into societal fears of aging, ugliness, frailty and lack of worthiness. It made me think about my own experience of getting older. Was I afraid of aging? What were my fears?

And, I was now experiencing growing older myself. I could see it and feel it — hairs turning grey, skin bumps, spots and lines, tooth and gum changes, muscle and joint changes, colder hands and feet with slowing circulation, vision changing as my arms stretched out as far as they could go (when did the text become so small?), metabolism slowing down. There were also reproductive changes; I was in the final years of child-bearing age. I was not going to be "fertile" for much longer and with that came a deep wave of emotional loss as I entered the beginning of the end of fertility.

I noticed others' reactions to my aging — men, women and transgender, young and old, younger and older — and found that people responded to my age in relation to their own. Forty was old to a 20-year-old and a babe to a 70-year-old. The first time I was addressed as "Ma'am" and not "Miss" was a bit of a shock. I had transitioned from one generation into the next. I was now middle-aged.

My feelings and attitudes about my grey hair shifted constantly, again in relation to others: when I noticed women who owned their grey hair with confidence or when others made comments about my grey hair: "You look distinguished", "I love the way your greys are growing in", "I love that look, like you have silver highlights." My hair stylist was a great listener, supporting my ambivalence about this hair transition and suggesting interesting ways to grow in my greys naturally. For several years I had highlighted and coloured my hair to cover my roots and my greys, and then I got tired of it — the expense, the time, the fakeness. It didn't make me look younger, and the truth was that I didn't want to be younger. Did it make me look healthier, sexier, prettier, and to whom? Who decided that, for me?

With fresh eyes I witnessed how retail, businesses and professionals prey upon vulnerable middle-aged people, taking advantage of their self-doubts, commercializing and monetizing their fears. I found myself feeling angry at the massive assault. None of it helped people to address their fears and anxieties, of course. It only masked them in super-hydrating moisturizers and hid them in luxurious real estate.

There was a deep chasm between my previous work environment with its inherent honouring of elders, and living and working in this weird world that age-shames. I was especially annoyed because I had experienced the age-friendly alternative and it was so much more wonderful, for everyone. But where did this ageist angst come from? I was fired up with a fierce curiosity, wanting to understand its roots and these fears of aging.

It dawned on me that we don't really talk about our own aging. In my years of schooling and working — in mental health and geriatric health — I cannot recall it. I don't remember being asked to explore my beliefs, experiences and feelings about aging. I do not have memories of discussing it with my classmates or colleagues. It is as though aging only happens to others — to patients, to clients, to "them," and not to all of us and our families.

Huh.

I had been a 20-something and 30-something clinician working in geriatric health care, and we hadn't discussed our own aging, our wrinkles, our feelings about getting old or becoming frail.

Wow. What is that about?

I realized that I had to do something that would transform my sense of frustrated helplessness. But, what? I wanted to create some kind of process or experience and began to brainstorm ideas. I wondered how to get people to talk about aging, especially their own. Because I want to feel the way I did as a 5-year-old, and live in a world where aging is not feared and where elders are valued, cared for and respected.

How *The Interview Project* began

My sense of frustration with age-shaming kept growing. I bristled when I heard ageist comments, read negative stereotypes, saw manipulative advertisements and outright meanness about getting old. Where was the respect? Where was the attempt to understand the complexity of what it is like to grow older?

As I wondered what I could do, I noticed a trend on social media of conversational interviews about various topics. I thought this format would work well and started to develop a structure that would be inclusive, participatory, collaborative and confidential.

This was the criteria and process for the interviews:
- The interviews were open to anyone over 21 years of age.
- They were about 60 minutes in length and conducted by phone or Skype.
- I audio-recorded each interview, then transcribed it myself to ensure confidentiality and privacy for the interviewee.
- I did some basic editing of the transcribed interview and sent it to the interviewee for their approval. They could delete, change or add whatever they wished. They also chose how they would be named with options ranging from their full name to an alias.
- The final version of their interview would be published on my blog, *Life Changes*, and available on the internet for anyone to read.

In 2010, I began to interview people about their thoughts and fears about aging. I shared the project widely: on social media, in my coaching newsletter, on my blog, in my courses and workshops, at virtual and real-life networking and social events. I extended the invitation to more than 2000 people.

My plan was to interview 100 participants in five years, by December 2015. One hundred seemed like a powerful number with credibility. Optimistically and naively, I really believed that I would find 100 individuals who would be ready to participate, thinking that the interviews would generate buzz. I had no idea that would be a problem.

The project was received with curiosity, caution and excitement. Several potential participants said that they found it too evocative, but people who were interested and ready to be interviewed contacted me.

I did a few interviews and noticed the participants gravitated to talking about death and dying, so I added specific questions on death and dying. At first I felt awkward and uncomfortable asking the interviewees about death. It got easier. The questions seemed to give people an opening to express their concerns, fears, and hopes. In fact, some people told me afterwards — once the digital recorder was turned off — that they felt relieved to have had a chance to talk about it.

I asked a friend, Patricia, to interview me because I wanted to experience the interview first-hand, from the other side: to know what it was like to be asked, to reflect on the questions and talk about them, and then to share my interview publicly. I wanted to find out how exposing and revealing it would be for me to talk about topics that are usually not talked about.

It was November 2010. Patricia came over to my home and I made us coffee. We were in my living room; she sat on the red sofa, I settled in the black armchair. She read over the sheet of paper with the interview questions, which I knew by heart, while I set up the digital recorder. She took me on a trip that I was not anticipating, sometimes veering off with a question that was not on the list, sometimes stopping to explore places that intrigued her. She asked me new questions that made me pause:

"Who is the Ruth today compared to the Ruth of 10 years ago, and 20 years ago?"

"How do you deal with loss during transitions, and in life?"

It's remarkable to read my interview responses from 2010. I'm six years older now, 50, and grateful to have those reflections captured, to know how I spoke, to see what was important for me then and what

I believed to be true. I can tell where in the interview I was not sure how to answer the questions — about dying, about death, about losses and heartbreak — and the edits I made so that I would be comfortable having my interview out in the world. It confirmed the importance of making the process confidential and private for the interviewee.

The interview project ran smoothly from 2010 until 2013. I completed thirty interviews with people from Canada, Ireland and the USA, who ranged in age from 20-something to 90 years old. Based on the information they shared, there was diverse culture, religion, race, and sexual orientation. Some participants were familiar to me, but most were acquaintances or complete strangers. Most of the interviewees seemed comfortable talking with me; they shared their experiences and beliefs in the way that you do with a trusted friend. It was important to me to create a respectful, curious, trusting connection, so that this conversation was possible.

In the middle of 2013, interest slowly dwindled. Once in a while someone poked their head in with an email or phone call to tell me they wanted to participate. It continued to fizzle and then, silence. Potential participants stopped showing up. I put out requests and call-outs for volunteers, but there were no inquiries. The project dried up completely. I didn't know what was wrong. I only had 30 interviews, nowhere near the 100 I was hoping for.

I didn't know what to do. I was in limbo and confused for what felt like a long time. I thought I was waiting for new interviewees to volunteer themselves. I thought some big, brilliant idea would spark me further. Nothing.

It was winter and this project was frozen. For months I felt stuck and alone in this barren hinterland of a project. I talked with friends and colleagues about how to make sense of the 30 interviews and tried to wrestle out some idea for how to move forward. Just when I decided to pull them together for a book, my dad became very ill. It was May 2014. I stepped away from the book idea in order to be with

THE INVITATION

my dad during the final months of his life.

In staying present to my experience, and to my dad's, my defenses were stripped away and I felt exposed and raw. He died in July 2014. I was surprised to discover that the interviewees had quietly prepared me. By listening to their experiences, I felt strengthened and inspired while I dealt with my father's illness, and needed to be his advocate as he died. They taught me what was possible for my family as he was dying. I had learned so much, including who and how I wanted to be as I grow older. Their stories, reflections and ideas impacted me deeply in ways that I did not anticipate.

It was only after my dad died that I knew. I had gotten stuck because I was waiting to experience the dying and death of someone I loved dearly. I now had lived experience to guide me forward.

And I also saw the taboo, the socially constructed silence that makes it so hard for us to be with death and dying. I could now understand, not only why people were reluctant to participate, but what was missing from the interviews. I, too, was under the spellbinding silence of the taboo. Even with all the conversations in my family about death and dying, there was still much unasked, unspoken and unknown. The taboo is powerful, prevalent and pervasive. I see how it enveloped this project, scaring people away from it, barricading them from participating.

The silence of the taboo haunts like a ghost, seeking out those who are most frightened of it, following closely those who deny and avoid it. Taboo clutches us with a tight grip on our throats, keeping us silent. Are we each aware of the taboo? Do we see how the taboo imprisons us, holding us hostage with our own fear?

Except for the 30 interviewees whom I found and who found me for this project. They were willing to step past their fears and explore the taboo.

I began to see the project with new eyes, and decided to work with what was happening, not against it. I shifted from thinking of the 30 interviews as, "Only 30?" to, "Oh wow, I got 30!" And I realized that this was 30 more than exist anywhere else.

It was at this point I realized that I wanted, and needed, to get back to the interviewees. After my dad died, my resolve for the project was renewed and I wanted to go further. I was ready to return with more questions, more understanding, more experience, more courage. Nothing felt off limits.

I contacted as many of the original 30 participants as I could locate and asked who wanted to move forward with me. We connected for a second conversation to clarify their stories and discussed whether their thoughts and beliefs had changed. I felt tender from grief, but also more knowledgeable about what questions to ask about dying and death, and how to ask them. These 16 interviews felt different to me. I continue to be changed by them.

Each conversation had a different quality: one was like we were on a fishing trip, another like having a late night chat in a college dorm room, another felt like picnicking in a park with family nearby, another like being by the seashore or having coffee in someone's kitchen. Each one felt unique.

This project became a book, with my thoughts about aging, dying and death included with the collection of 16 interviews. Each one was storied collaboratively with the interviewee. They are filled with the rawness of being human, real-life inspiration and the wisdom of our collective humanity.

THE INVITATION

❧

2

EMILY'S STORY

Emily is a 78-year-old woman who has lived alone for the last thirty years, is still healthy and active, still working as an editor and tutor, still loving life and looking ahead to more of it. Emily has a daughter, a son and six grandchildren, and has come to learn more than ever that the love of family and friends is all that really matters. She has written books in the past and is writing her memoir now, which she plans to publish and give to her children. Emily volunteers at a hospice and a library. She enjoys gardening, making fabric art, going to movies and taking long walks with friends.

As Emily shares her story with me, I feel as though we are strolling along a forest trail. It's mid-autumn and the leaves are turning their brilliant hues of copper, flame red and burnt orange.

To me, growing older is simply accepting certain natural, incremental changes that occur as the years go by. I don't feel much different now than I did twenty or thirty years ago because I'm lucky enough to have stayed healthy all my life. When I was young I used to think that 60 was it, that you were really over the hill. Then I reached 60 and thought, "Wow! This is great! I'm feeling good and not looking too bad either." I think, for me, hitting 70 was when I realized I wasn't young anymore.

I had some facial surgery a few years ago to remove skin cancer

EMILY'S STORY

on my nose, and the surgery was more traumatic than I'd expected. The bleeding couldn't be stopped, and I had to be rushed to a plastic surgeon, who re-stitched the incision. Then a few days later he did skin-graft surgery, and afterward I looked like I'd been in a prizefight. My whole face was bruised and red, my nose was huge. I looked like something out of a horror movie. I got very depressed and thought, "Well, I'll have to get used to being ugly for the rest of my life." Miraculously though, my nose healed, and three months after the surgery I looked like my old self again. But it was one of those times when something totally unexpected and scary happened that made me feel my age. It heightened my awareness of how I look to the world. I didn't realize how important that was because I don't think I'm vain, but I'm not unattractive, and boy, was I ugly for a while! I felt very self-conscious about going out in public, so that taught me something about myself. For the most part, I think I've aged well. I am 78, but people tell me I look younger. How should I know? I look at myself, and to me, that's what 78 looks like.

One's self-image can be so different from reality. Recently I was staying in a hotel where the bathroom had a huge mirror and bright fluorescent lights, and it shocked me to see all the wrinkles and protruding bones I hadn't seen before. At home I have older, softer lighting that isn't so harsh, and I think I'll keep it that way. But most of the time, in my daily life, I'm unaware of my age. Then a knee aches or my mind goes blank on a word and I think, "Oh, no wonder! I'm old."

A year after the nose surgery, more cancer was found on my chin. It took two surgeries to remove all the cancer cells and now I have a visible scar that runs up my chin to my bottom lip. At first it bothered me a lot, but now I'm used to it. It's part of me. Part of who I am now. In a way I've become proud of my scars because each one tells a meaningful story.

A year and a half ago I found a large lump in my breast (stage 1 cancer) and decided to have a mastectomy. A friend took me to the hospital for the surgery and I stayed just one night. A few days later I felt well enough to drive my 89-year-old brother to a restaurant, where we had lunch together. I felt tired but otherwise surprisingly good. Because of my age, and because no cancer was found in the lymph nodes, my doctor and I decided against chemotherapy or radiation, though I will take medication for the rest of my life. My recovery has been so easy that I often forget I'm a cancer survivor.

Now that I'm older I'm willing to relax more and not feel guilty about it because I know I can't go-go-go all the time the way I used to. It isn't physically possible. I'm slowing down, so why not accept it and enjoy looking out the window or taking a quiet walk, not feeling that I have to accomplish something all the time? That's one great blessing of old age. Taking time to listen to people, talk to people, not having to hurry through experiences, but just soak it all in. Now I can appreciate single moments, joyful moments.

It's interesting to me how I used to think that old people's feelings must diminish along with their minds and bodies. But I'm discovering that's not true at all; my emotions are as strong as ever, and I'm thankful for that. It surprises me that I can be as worried, as happy, as surprised, as sad, as shocked as I ever was. That doesn't change. I don't worry as much about my children, though, as I did when they first set out on their own. I've learned to accept that they're adults, that they have their own work and their own lives. But don't think I've flung all my worries aside! Grandchildren have given me a whole new set of things to worry about.

The most challenging transition in my life was my divorce at age 46. I'd thought about leaving for maybe ten years before I had the courage to actually say out loud to my husband, "I don't love you, and I have to leave this marriage." It was scary to actually say the words. There'd been no abuse, no cheating; we'd just drifted apart and were no longer friends. Leaving was painful and difficult, but I knew it was right. I'd desperately wanted my freedom, but didn't realize how scary it would be to actually have it. I had to learn to live independently, and of course there were lonely times. Friends helped me through the first few months. As if divorce wasn't enough to handle, my mother and sister both died unexpectedly the same year. That was definitely the hardest year of my life.

I have strong spiritual feelings, but I can't say that religion got me through that period because I'm not religious and I don't belong to a church. I do have deep connections with something in the universe that helps me through tough times, but I couldn't get through them without close, loving connections to other people.

The biggest surprise of my life came soon after my divorce, when I fell in love with a woman — and boy, did I fall hard. For two years we lived together as "roommates" because being gay was not accepted then the way it is now, and we had to be very secretive about our relationship. That was a very happy time for me, and I was devastated when my partner eventually left me. Looking back, I have no regrets because the experience taught me so much about myself. For several years after the relationship ended I was confused about my sexuality. Was I gay? Straight? Bisexual? As time went on, I came to realize that I felt no attraction whatsoever to women. Men? Yes. That answered my question.

In my 70s, I was attracted to a man who was five years younger than I was. I realized that if I were in my 40s, 50s, or even my 60s, five years difference between us would seem like nothing. I was uncomfortable with it, but he just laughed and said it didn't matter. The problem was, after being in this country for several months he moved back to India, and neither of us could afford to travel. We were in close touch for two years via Skype, but eventually the romantic side of our relationship petered out and morphed instead into a valued friendship.

Falling in love at 70 was wonderful: having that old rush, those romantic feelings, that physical desire. I didn't know that could happen in one's mid-70s, and I discovered that it can. Now there are so many other things that interest me more than pursuing a relationship. It's just nature; it's the way it is. I'm sad that I don't have someone I've been with for many years, and I envy couples who are still very close and will grow old together. There is something enviable about that, but not having it is not something I dwell on. I have treasured friends, good health and, most of the time, a happy, fulfilling life.

One of the most difficult things about getting older is that friends and family members are getting ill and dying. My best friend from childhood died five years ago. I have friends with arthritis, with heart problems, one who has double vision now and can't drive. It's sad when these things happen to people you care about. Fortunately, I still have friends my age and older who are in good health and lead active lives. What I know now that I didn't know when I was young is that friendships grow more precious over the years. They need to be nurtured and never taken for granted.

My parents were 38 and 40 when I was born, and they both aged well, at least physically. My mother, however, didn't age well emotionally. She became extremely depressed in her late 60s. As I was growing up, she was the kind of mother who was happy and fun to be with. She loved everything about being a mother and raising a family. Her first signs of depression came after the four of us left home and she no longer felt needed because her interests had all revolved around the family. One day, at age 68, she woke up on the floor after having a mini stroke, and from then on she was fearful about going out and driving and doing things alone. I think the combination of losing her family and fearing more strokes was what caused her severe depression that lasted for fifteen years until her death at 82.

My father was a doctor of internal medicine who practiced until he was in his 70s. He loved being with people and he loved working. After retirement, he became director of post-graduate education at a large hospital, helping to educate interns and residents. The way he kept going, helping others and doing work he loved, was a great example for me. At 85, after my mother died, Dad married a woman who was 82 and had never married. She had been a doctor, too, and they had known each other in medical school many years before. Years later they met at a conference and decided they didn't want to be alone in their final years, so they got married. Not long afterward, they were both hurt in a car accident, and I went to live with them, since I had recently divorced and was free to move. Then Dad got multiple myeloma, and I became the caretaker for both of them. That turned out to be a wonderfully rewarding experience and I'm so grateful that I was with my dad in his last years.

My father was remarkable in the way he dealt with dying. Toward the end of his illness, he often said to me, "I don't understand why I'm still here. Really, it's time for me to go. I'm ready." But his constitution was so strong that he just hung on. When the time finally came for his passing, it was very peaceful. I knew the moment his soul left him. It was in his eyes. Suddenly there was nothing there. Moments before, he had been reaching upward, looking up at something the rest of us couldn't see. And then there was nothing — his eyes were empty. It was a remarkable experience for me — a peaceful one because I knew he wanted this to happen. As a result, I have no fear of death because I know, through him, that we are going to a better place.

Last year I became my brother's caretaker and his power of attorney, a job that involves a great deal of time and energy. I've had to cut way back on my editing work in order to take him to doctor appointments, help with his banking, do his laundry, and keep him company. I don't live with him, but we live in the same city and I check on him every day. Because he realizes that caring for him means less income for me, he allows me to withdraw enough from his bank account each month to pay my bills. His general health is fairly good, but his memory is bad, he is often confused, and he has problems with personal hygiene. I feel, and his children feel, that it's time for him to move to an assisted living facility. However, he is strongly opposed to the idea and insists that he wants to die in his own house. I can see that this is going to be a struggle, but I know that a decision will have to be made soon.

I've been a volunteer at a hospice for about four years, where I visit with people who know they haven't long to live. Their calm acceptance of their situation and the joy they take in whatever time is left to them surprises and humbles me. I was on good terms with death before starting this work or I wouldn't have taken it on. What constantly amazes me is how comfortable most of these people are with the knowledge that they have only a short time left to live.

I can't honestly say that I'm ready to die or that I want to die, but I don't have any great fears concerning death. I've written a will, I've made arrangements for my body to be donated to a medical school or hospital, and I've let my children know about my choices. I want everything to cost as little as possible because I know how expensive funerals can be. So I don't want a funeral and I don't want a casket.

Dying can be a long process, and I only hope that my care won't create difficulties for my family. I do fear being incapacitated and having to depend on someone else for my care. I'm a very independent person and hate the thought of being a burden to anyone, even though I've come to see that that can be a kind of natural progression. I've taken care of my father, I'm taking care of my brother, and in many ways that's been a good thing for all of us. What I hope is that I'm lucid enough to tell my loved ones goodbye, then pass away in my sleep, quietly, like my mother. However, until that time comes, I'm going to forget about dying and concentrate on living the best life I can, one day at a time.

3

BRAD'S STORY

Brad is a 29-year-old South African who moved to Canada when he was 15. He studied Health Policy in university before working as a project manager in a large educational hospital. He enjoys cooking, baking and, most of all, travelling. Brad has four older brothers, including two half-brothers, and the oldest is 45. He loves his partner, great running shoes, warm weather and travelling.

Talking together, we both notice how it feels like we're having a late night conversation in a university dorm room, and we're talking about saving the world in our little bubble.

A few things happened in my family that made me think more about dying. My aunt, who is relatively young in her mid-60s, had a stroke. She was jogging 5 to 10 km every day and now she requires 24-hour care. She is not able to look after herself. Events like that make me think. It's not like typical aging, where there is increased care over a number of years, where someone was completely independent and needs some help with housework as it gets more challenging, and then eventually transitions to living in a place that provides nursing care. I've experienced having a grandmother getting older and going through a more natural course of aging. She was in her 80s so it seemed to make sense, whereas in my aunt's situation it was not a natural progression.

Also, my half-brother was involved in a car accident where the passenger he was driving with was killed. He was injured pretty heavily. It makes me think about my parents and myself in those situations, what I want for myself and how to ensure that my parents and I communicate what we want. You know (laughing) when you think about it, it seems really silly not to have sat down and had that conversation, given that someone in our family has had this happen to them. You'd think we'd sit down and say, "What if this happened to one of us?" Because we're immediate family, of course we would be responsible for looking after one another in that situation.

My parents feel that things should be in place when they're older, for example, long-term disability insurance and sufficient retirement savings. They want me to have the freedom to look after my own family when I get older and they'll ensure that they'll be okay, financially. I think that's how their parents saw it as well — that it is the parents' responsibility to look after themselves financially as much as possible and not the children's issue. But what's still missing is the emotional piece, sitting down and having that emotional discussion, not the practical talk about coverage and financial issues. Right now would be a perfect time to discuss it because my parents and siblings wouldn't be offended or feel we would be implying that it's time to send you "off to the ice floe now." I've had that discussion with my boyfriend, it's easy for me in that situation, I don't know why! Maybe that's the best way to approach it, to be matter-of-fact and say what I want the limits of my care to be, and that I'd be happy if they'd make that decision for me one day if they had to. I think my generation is not accustomed to talking with our parents about our emotions and things that don't have a practical purpose. You have to make that conscious decision to just sit down and have that chat.

Just before we left South Africa my grandmother became quite unwell. She was always an old woman, she wasn't sprinting across the room any time I can remember but she lived independently in her own apartment. I remember that my mom got a call saying that she had to go see her mother because she was in hospital. It must have been a critical event because it was very sudden. I'm not sure what the illness was, but all at once she looked very different, like a patient in a facility rather than a resident in a retirement community. She had to move into the assisted-living community and eventually needed full-time care. That was something that I was unprepared for. I think as a child you don't anticipate seeing someone you know age suddenly. Before, she had been a very stern and confident "this was how it was going to be done" lady — my mother would sometimes say how "Grandma wouldn't have allowed that" — but afterward my grandmother could not remember who we were; she couldn't speak. It was a complete change in her: she needed assistance, she needed someone to take a tissue to her face after eating, she needed help eating. That was my first experience with aging and seeing someone reach end-of-life stages.

I do feel uncomfortable saying my age when I haven't thought about it for several months and a friend says, "Oh yeah, it's gonna be your birthday soon, how old will you be?" When I tell them my age, I think, "Oh crap, I can't believe I'm 25!" I have four older brothers, so I've had four other people go through the age that I'm about to turn. I think of myself as too young to be 25, even though to many people it is very young. It's surprising to all of a sudden be that age. I don't know if it's because 25 is the middle of the second decade, but I feel like now I'm truly an adult. I should be getting into the real world and have a proper job, start thinking about a house and maybe kids, so it wakes me up and makes me realize that I'm older than I think I am.

The best thing about aging is the ability to decide your direction — your career, lifestyle, interests — and to acquire your independence. I see myself planning a trip and I realize it's a "symptom" of getting older. I now have the ability to travel the world and do it on my own terms. I'm less dependent on what my parents are saying or what my family is doing. As you get older and acquire more wealth (it always seems to come back to money), you're able to choose where you want to live, what you want to do next, where you want to visit. Those things that seemed to be so ingrained in my childhood, I now have the independence to do away with, if I choose, and the repercussions are not as bad as it seemed. I realized that going to church or being religious wasn't something I valued. I have the experience of attending a religious institution and have a little bit of wisdom that allows me to see what is important to me. It's interesting to me that my parents went through a similar transition because they also attend a new church where there's more of a community. Everyone in my family went through a re-prioritization of our values, as we grew older. It's also funny how my parents treat me as I age — if they see me doing something that previously they weren't happy with, like drinking or swearing, suddenly it becomes acceptable, it's okay. I can tell a rude joke at home, something I could never get away with; it's funny how now my parents will laugh.

One of the biggest experiences that greatly contributes to how I view aging was when I was in high school and did a co-op placement with Toronto Ambulance. For four months I went around with a crew, and what I found most disturbing was when we saw that an elderly person was not provided care options. I'd see a person who had lived their life; like many, they'd had their challenges and paid their dues. I expected a 70- or 80-year-old person would have earned sufficient respect so that they wouldn't have to be in a situation where their care wasn't on their terms.

There was a specific incident when we went to a retirement residence. The guy had to go into an ambulance to go somewhere (for treatment), so he needed to be readied to leave the facility. I guess the caregivers hadn't gotten him ready and he needed his diaper changed. I thought, "This poor guy has to watch us discuss what needs to be done to him while he's sitting in bed." So the facility staff start to change his diaper right then in front of us. We're saying, "We'll walk outside while you do that," to give him some privacy and dignity. He wasn't able to direct his care or say, "I need to be cleaned and changed so that I can head out," like anyone at any age would do. It made me realize that you really need to have options and control over how you will live when you get older, and those options come from having the finances to choose. One of my greatest fears is that one day I would be in a position where I'd be unable to communicate what I want for myself and be subjected to people doing the best they could, but it not being consistent with what I want.

I've thought about opening up an organization whose goal is to help people who have some fear, like I do, about not just where they are when they die, but how they get there, and to have control of that situation as it approaches. I think everyone deep down wants to do something that they have a yearning for, and this would be something for me that would meet that goal. It could start small. It's about making an impact in our own lives and also having a wider impact, perhaps leaving a legacy that we can feel proud of.

I don't think about how I want to die but I do think about how I'd like to live just before that point. My biggest concern is more about the process rather than the actual event. For example, if someone has a sudden event that is debilitating but they don't physically pass away and yet they're left very much without a life. I wouldn't want that for my family members or myself. Now, with medicine the way it is, there's a very good chance of dying becoming an ongoing process instead of an event where someone dies in their sleep. I don't think that happens too often anymore.

It seems like it's not acceptable to choose how long we're going to let someone live unless it's clear within the medical context that the person is brain-dead. To some degree, I disagree with doing everything you can to ensure a person lives, however, at the same time, I understand that within the ethics of science you can't NOT do everything. Because who makes that choice? You can't rely on a medical professional to make that choice. I wouldn't want anyone within my family to go through that, to enter that ethical struggle. I would really hope that when death came for my family that it was a sudden event. I think it would be very difficult for the person who passes away to go through the process of enduring a slow death within a facility. I'd rather mourn someone's death than mourn them not having the capacity to look after their own life.

THE INVITATION

4

Mariana's Story

Mariana was born in Romania, lived in Paris, New York City and now Toronto, which is where she calls home. She always loved the sciences and received her master's degree in science, then followed up later with a master's degree in engineering. She is a 68-year-old professional woman who, with all her career successes, including receiving an award from the prime minister for her work, values her three children as her most important achievement. She loves being a grandmother to her two grandsons and three granddaughters, who range in age from 3 to 11. She does all kinds of work: volunteer work, quiet philanthropic work and creative work. She enjoys reading gossip magazines, loves earrings, shoes, beautiful music and when people succeed in whatever they want to be.

Talking with Mariana, I feel like we are in an old college library surrounded by dark wooden bookcases stacked with books, green glass-shaded table lamps with polished brass switches, comfy brown leather chairs, worn velvet sofas, and padded Persian rugs. She sits on a purple velvet sofa, her strong voice animated in the soft darkness of the library.

When people see me they start talking slower with me, but I pull out the "by the way, I have two Master degrees and I'm pretty bright," and then they stop. When people notice you're a bit older, they answer back with a very minimalistic-type explanation. You have to stick up for your rights! There is a lot of ageism going on. When people say, "You're a little old lady, you don't know what you're talking about," I get really upset. People defer to a younger person; they think you don't know as much, when in fact as we grow older we accumulate experience and wisdom. I notice this ageist attitude in North America towards old people, that they're not as active or as important and that bothers me. When people see that you're older they treat you like a second-class citizen. I'm going to start a revolt on that. I think it's the way you handle that problem. You can tell people, "Just because I'm older than you doesn't give you the right to treat me this way." I think people need to be put in their place.

To me, old means not being able to walk as fast and do as many things as I used to do. I'm a Type A personality, and the minute I get up, I go-go-go. I'm still fast, but now I notice that I need to catch my breath when I walk quickly. I tell my daughter for whom I do a lot of babysitting, "Honey, I think I'm too tired to do it." So maybe that's one way that aging comes about. As you get older, I think you become gentler, not so tough on yourself. You accept those wrinkles and say, "I've earned them." You have a certain peace of mind. I do.

I learned from my parents, who were Holocaust survivors, how to overcome hurdles. We are survivors. You have to learn to be a survivor. I've had a lot of hurdles in my life. Going back to school when I was 40 to get my Masters in Engineering made me even tougher. My husband was dying, I had three kids, my parents weren't able to help me financially, and I still went back to school. When a professor told me that I didn't have the brains, I said to him that he should get lost, that he was a stupid idiot! We managed all right and I got one contract after another, then two full-time job offers. My late husband used to say if Clint Eastwood saw me, he'd run the other way!

I also learned from my grandpa, who gave us a lot of love and power. He used to tell all the boys, "Go away! You're not good enough for my granddaughters!" From him I learned the power of being older, being wiser. Now I talk with my grandkids about women's liberation. I try to teach my granddaughters that they can punch the boys in the nose if the boys bug them! My grandkids give me a lot of new horizons, new sprigs of youth and wisdom. My role is to educate them about Judaism, and be there for them. I love that they tell me their little secrets when their parents are working and I'm there with them. I'm an extra ear for them. It's a special relationship.

Retirement was the most challenging transition in my life. I had a very stressful, high-powered job — the senior safety officer in a division of the federal government. I was on-call at night and very busy. I haven't had much leisure because I've always worked hard. The adjustment was hard at the beginning. It was hard not having a job to go to where I could practice my skills and feel useful. I was very down, doubtful, and thought a lot about whether I was still worthwhile.

When you work it's like you're on a centrifuge, round and round, and when you retire it's like a violin that you tune. You have to find out how much to tune your own violin and I think I found it. I had to find things I enjoyed, that give me a sense of being useful. I have to give myself permission to do things that I like. I don't have to run as much. Before I didn't have time to go to the washroom! Now I have time: to organize my life, organize my closet, take time with how I dress, put my financial things in order. I can just sit in my condo and see the entire city, take in the beauty and nature. Just taking a moment to do that and think quietly.

I took some very good courses about retirement, which have helped me: how to save for retirement, how to become closer to your family and friends who are becoming the centre of your life now, how to have interests.

I realized that it's like having money in the bank — all this experience and help that I've given people: that counts for something. And that's being invested into me, in fun now. I realized I can practice my wisdom in other ways. Now I'm becoming more artsy, more creative. Working before in sciences and engineering I was very analytical. Now

I can let my hair down! I wear funky clothes, write poetry. I wrote my autobiography and sent it to friends. I love to sing and dance with my grandkids and enjoy music concerts.

I have to make sure that I have my bag, the bag that needs to be filled: closeness with my kids, my finances to be there to look after me when I get older, certain trips I want to take, being kind to people and being with people whose company I really enjoy. I feel at home when there are bright people around me. When I went through tough times, some people were not there for me so I dropped them as friends. I sure appreciated the ones who were there.

Through retirement I discovered I need my space and I like my own company. At the beginning it was a little scary. I didn't realize how happy I can be on my own. I guess it's because I'm independent. I can do things I want, when I want to. If I feel like walking naked around the apartment I can. If I don't want to do something, I don't have to. I rented a house in Florida for a month; it was the first time I did it on my own and went on my own — that was a big accomplishment for me. I rented a car and drove myself around. Just renting the house and getting about, that was a big achievement.

In my building there are older people, but many of them have caregivers. I plan to take good care of myself so I won't have to have a caregiver. I try to stay away from them because I'm so young at heart. I plan to live here until I'm pretty old, but I am looking around for other options. If I get very ill, I've made provisions for a nurse to come here and look after me, so that I won't be turfed out to a nursing home. I still consider myself young. I'm 68. I think my kids are leaving it up to me and when I'm ready I can contact them. If there is something I need to talk to my son about, I'll let him know that I need to chat with him. He knows I'm tough. I think when I turn 75 I'll talk about aging with them.

I never think about dying. When it comes, it comes. It's a part of life. I plan to go to heaven and party! I would like to be a race-car driver, but that's not a safe thing to do. I don't fear death and dying at all. I think

I've done a lot in my life. I've achieved whatever I wanted to achieve.

In my family we don't talk that much about death and dying because what's more important is the quality of that time we have. We share a joke or news of what's happening. My younger son is a busy doctor and his wife is a doctor too, so when I meet with them I make sure they are okay and they make sure everything is okay with me.

Sometimes I tell them, "You know, I'm getting a little older guys." And they say, "Oh, no, no, Mum! You're a spring chicken!" I think my kids don't want to accept that their mother is getting older. They want to see me active and nicely dressed because that's what I showed them my whole life. I'm travelling to Florida and to China, so they are proud that I keep doing my own thing and that I speak up. The worry I do have about dying is that I don't want to be a burden to my kids. I hope my death will be easy and fast. I hope I have another life on the other side.

❧

5

JOEL'S STORY

Joel is a 73-year-old retired businessman, husband, father of six and grandfather of seven. The oldest grandchild just turned 21. He grew up in Canada and now lives in New York City, his dream come true. He loves travelling, culture, theatre, music and clever writing. He does air force exercises and stretches in the shower, like his grandmother did for 40 years, so that he stays flexible and can enjoy his life. As he says, "You don't need an outfit; the shower is there and the heat makes it easier to move your muscles."

Talking with Joel, I feel like we are in a hip New York diner. It is dimly lit with art deco windows and mirrors; there is a buzz from the other diners. Joel is an engaging talker, he says he feels like he's rambling, but I assure him it is all captivating.

My mother is very young in her attitude. She's my role model. She's 96 and she still golfs, drives, and goes to theatre all the time. When she visited New York City a couple of years ago for my daughter's graduation, she walked at least a mile every day. She went to see a play, the Book of Mormon, which is certainly not geared to people who are 90 years old. She loved it and said it was terrific! She's aware of modern culture and participates in it. She's an example to me of someone who is not old, and she's living exactly the way I would like to if I ever get to her age. She eats healthily and has done so all her life. She's lucky, too. It pays off in terms of what she's able to do now and how she can enjoy her life.

My mother's mother lived to 106. Her attitude was like my mother's; she always ate nutritious foods long before there was talk about being healthy. She never jogged; she just had a busy, active life. And they both had to make new friends because their long-time friends had died. If you get old enough, some of your friends die, people move away, the world changes, and if you aren't open to change, your world diminishes. It keeps diminishing and diminishing. All you're left with is saving old things, and talking about old things and thinking about how things were wonderful before.

My grandmother always said the "good old days" were not the good old days, and that's quite true. There were no good old days. Consider a hundred years ago, when Jews were living in ghettos, black people were slaves and gay people were killed. And there were no medicines and antibiotics. So, there are no "good old days."

I believe that you can't age well if you don't spend social time with people. The value of real friendship is so important; real friends are your chosen family. You need people around you; you need to be socially engaged. Good mental health is important as you age, there's no question. And if you want people around you, you can't complain about what's wrong. My grandmother never did that. We always wondered what was physically bothering her because she never said anything. She never complained about her aches and pains. People don't want to hear that unless it's a bunch of old people sitting around saying the same thing.

The harder things about getting older happen in increments, and dealing with them is about self-acceptance. I don't like fighting those things. Recently I visited Toronto, the city where I grew up, and attended an event with my contemporaries. They seemed like old people to me, even the way they looked, the way they dressed, their hair — many are fixed in time. Some people have their heyday and stay there. They have the hairstyle that they had in a certain year, thought it suited them and never changed it. I used to see moustaches on men — thinking what year did they get that one? I think it's foolish for a man to dye his hair — you think you'll look younger, but you don't look younger, you just look like you're the same age but you've dyed your hair. Or worrying about baldness or comb-overs or anything else like that. Or getting plastic surgery to make yourself look younger. I always say I'd be the first in line and pay the money if it actually made me younger — that would be great! But to pretend you look younger when it doesn't actually make you any younger? It doesn't restore anything that really matters. Your age is obvious in the way you move and in many other ways, despite your face being unlined.

When I was young, particularly as a teenager, I was whoever my friends expected me to be. I had several different close friends, and I was somebody different for each of them. I didn't have confidence in expressing my opinions, which are pretty strong, if I thought I would offend people. As I've gotten older, I'm not afraid of stating them. I say it in a nice way, but I don't care whether someone agrees with me or not, or if they're shocked or whatever. So, along with aging, there is speaking your mind more freely. And not wasting time on things that aren't important. Not spending time with people you don't like or don't want to be with. Not spending time out of obligation where there is none; time is precious. These seem to be some of the good things that can come with aging and maturity — mainly self-acceptance.

I was 19 when I got married the first time and the relationship was unsatisfying. The most challenging thing for me was coming out as gay without understanding it, and dealing with the effects of it on my children. Leaving the marriage was very, very difficult. Even though I wanted to leave. But leaving when I had four young children . . .

When the marriage ended I was 30, and I actually thought that 30 was so old that my life was basically over. I thought that whatever happened with the new relationship, well there couldn't be that much of a future because I was already 30 years old. Isn't that funny? I was starting a whole new life that I didn't really understand, and just going with it emotionally. There was no pattern to follow, there were no role models, I just went with my heart without using my brain, which I've done most of the time! I always say that the best, most important, decisions you make are made not with the brain, but with your heart, taking a leap and taking a chance. At first everything was a mystery. We had fantasized about sharing a life together, but we'd never heard of anyone else doing it. It was a time of tremendous turmoil. The emotions we experienced were so strong that they felt like a tornado. But there was no choice. A life together was all we wanted, so we just kept going. We just saw it through.

When I meet young, gay people socially now and I talk to them, I say, "You can't understand this, that in the early 1970s I'd never heard of two gay people living together. It wasn't even an option." I understood about being attracted, but I never, never . . . I actually didn't know that two men kissed, you know that? So it was pioneering in my own way.

The day I moved out and ended my first marriage, I called my now-husband and said, "I'm moving out today."

He said, "Oh! Do you want to move in here?"

I said, "Oh, okay."

We never knew, never had an idea that we could set up a life together. We just did it! But it was nothing we'd seen or read about or heard of. We just decided that if someone didn't invite the two of us somewhere together, we wouldn't go. We didn't announce it to anybody and it happened that everything followed. Then, of course, we got strong.

When I left my marriage that day, a close relative said to me, "Do you think this new relationship will last?"

I said to him, "Well, I'd be foolish to say so, to make a statement after I'm just coming out of an 11-year relationship that didn't last, but I hope it lasts as long as I want it to last. That's all I can say."

He said to me, "Well, you know that no homosexual relationship has ever lasted more than six months."

So I said, "Well where did you get your information?"

He said, "I don't know."

As soon as I got home to my husband, I said, "We're going to make it to six months, and I'm going to send him a card when it's six months and one day!" But he didn't let me do it. Who knew?! And we've been together 43 years! It's funny, of course, now people get married in their 30s and have children in their 40s. I always liked to do things early! Yes, I used to think 30 was "It" — you were already over the hill.

That was the biggest risk I took. When I left my marriage and came out as gay, it was a big issue whether or not to tell the children. My ex-wife's doctor said that I was "polymorphous perverse" and that the children must never know (remember it was the early 1970s), and that if they ever found out it would just destroy them. So, for a while I didn't tell. There was no awareness around it, there were no TV shows talking about it, there was nothing. I didn't want to take a chance and risk destroying my children, but I was feeling very badly. We never said there was a relationship between my husband and me. I've always wanted to be truthful, and I never wanted to hide things or lie, especially to my children. It took a number of years, and then after a while I realized I didn't care what that doctor thought; I didn't believe it. I told my eldest, and once I told her I thought I should tell the next child, and once I started with two, I went to three and four, and told them all. Those were difficult days — there was no support or anybody guiding me. Probably my instincts were pretty good. Ultimately, I believe that we're just humans, basically all the same no matter what the variation.

Adopting children was another big risk as well. And it was a jump. It was starting all over. First of all, I never planned on having any more children. I wanted to have kids when I was young, so that I would have adult children when I was still young and could enjoy them. But my husband had never had any and it meant a lot to him, so that was why I did it. I thought I couldn't deny him something so basic, if that was what he wanted. And with that too — we were gay, we didn't know any other gay people who had children, and so we were again at the beginning of that movement. Our family was interracial, and that was another factor. People used to stop us on the street for three reasons — being gay, being men and being interracial.

The whole thing, all aspects of this are about love, including being an interracial family. The nicest part is that all my children became close to each other, and that was what I wanted, that was my fantasy (for them). That's really important to my husband and me, it gives us a lot of security, to know that our two kids have a solid family that loves them and that they love. When you have children, seeing them settled, having lives of their own and being independent, that is an important one. I always thought how exciting it would be to have a grandchild, but I realized after I had that grandchild, who is now 21, that the most exciting part for me wasn't having a grandchild, but seeing my child have a child. It was more important to watch my children, see them have their lives, relating to their children. I love looking at my children with their children — it's really special.

The most important thing is my relationship with my husband, without a doubt. It's above everything else, a mile above everything else. It's very precious. I count every moment of it because I'm aware that at some point it will end, either for him or for me, because one of us is going to go. We talk about that a lot. I guess I've realized what's important in my life and what's not important, and what other people think isn't particularly important unless they're people I really love. I think I'm very lucky, but one thing I can say about myself is that when an opportunity presented itself, I took it, and I acted on it. You have to take advantage of opportunity. You have to actively be open to things and when they are there, take that chance.

There's a timeline, and I'm getting to the end of the timeline, which is unfathomable. Unfathomable. I guess it is about still having a mother, too. When I was younger I looked at (generational) lines like a cliff and the generations were lined up. For a long time I had a grandmother, too, so I had two people ahead of me. Now I have one ahead of me, so I guess when my mother dies, that cliff will be looming closer, but right now there's a buffer. She's a buffer.

I had a lot of trouble with dying, a tremendous fear of dying, until I was 30-something. I couldn't work it out. The fear was about coming to terms with the fact that I wouldn't be here anymore.

I think some of my adjustment with dying has to do with having children and grandchildren. There's a sense that I'm not going to be here, but also a sense of continuity in my mind. My dad died young; he was 66. And I thought he was old when he died. We were in the car with him when he died. He was driving and we were headed to Epcot, in Florida. It had just opened and he didn't want to stay overnight. He asked my husband, Michael, and me if we would accompany him for the day, and we said, "Sure!" He drove the car and when we were about 20 miles away, he just (snaps fingers). It was like turning off a light switch. My mother, who is a very pragmatic, practical person, was in shock, grabbed onto the steering wheel and pulled onto the median strip. And he died there. I loved my father and I was very close to him, the closest of all the four children. I remember thinking at the time, "Well, he was 66 and he had a full life." That's what I thought, and I was 42. Of course now I think, "Sixty-six! He was young!"

My mother was a good example for me after my father died. My parents had a fantastic relationship. They were close friends, shared all kinds of interests together, and always spent their time together. When my father died, my mother never felt sorry for herself. She felt that she was lucky for what she had, not for what she had lost. It is like the embryo of a chicken before it's born, and the egg. You have all this nourishment stored up from what a relationship gives you, and then when you're without it, you feed off it. Of course, I've never been put to the test but, if I'm the survivor, I hope that's how I'll look at it.

I don't want to dwell on it like I did when I was younger. I just want to enjoy the present and be in the moment, enjoy the moments I have, and certainly not waste them worrying. As bad as anything can be, I'd rather know it than not know it. I don't want surprises in life. And, of course, I'd like my death to be sudden. It would be wonderful to know I'd die in three months, and then in three months (snaps fingers), lights out! Quality of life is the key. Of course we do talk all the time that if I'm like "that" I'm going to shoot myself or walk off the cliff or go off onto an ice floe — the culturally acceptable thing to do. I don't want to suffer. I don't want to be a burden to anybody else. We always say shoot me if I get to a certain stage, but I could live with uncertainty and incapacities as long as I could move around or do something — as soon as I couldn't look after myself, I don't want to be alive.

At some point I realized, "Listen, there's no 'if' about it! It's not IF I die, it's WHEN I die!" So I decided I have to make the most of it and try to have the highest quality of life that I can, to find pleasure while I can and not let time pass without knowing it. I don't want to die, that's for sure; I'm having too much fun.

THE INVITATION

❦

6

Gabriele's Story

Gabriele arrived in Canada from Germany at the age of seven. She explored fashion design before becoming an administrative assistant, and has lived and worked in Toronto most of her life. She is 67, but how she feels in age varies day-to-day. Gabriele loves hats, books, the sound of the surf, working out at the gym, her friends and travelling. She is grateful for her good health and the relationship she holds with her adult son.

Chatting with Gabriele feels like we are sipping tea (with brandy) at an outdoor patio as the sun is setting. Two women engaged in a deep conversation some moments, giggling together at other moments.

One of the things I've come to realize is that I have to accept the fact that I'm aging and that my physical capabilities are changing. That happened in my 40s, when I needed bifocal eyeglasses, and also with the end of menstruation. I used to complain about it — that time of the month was never easy for me because of pain and other symptoms — but once it was no longer going to be there, it felt like a loss. I was used to it and in some strange way wanted to keep it, knowing that it was the finale, that I've spent all these years trying not to get pregnant and it wasn't going to be a concern any more. That was a difficult adjustment, but I had to accept that it was another change. It was something

I could not have anticipated. I didn't have friends that I could discuss that with. There were other changes in my 50s, but not so much as the end of menstruation.

I don't have a problem with saying my age, and — I'm being brutally honest here — it's because people don't believe me. So it's sort of a compliment, but I'll probably get to the point where I look as old as I am chronologically. I don't fear aging. I'm trying to be amused by all these changes! Sometimes I say, "Oh wow, this is what's going to happen to my face over here!" Or, "Oh wow! This is going to wrinkle!" or, "Wow, I didn't know that was going to happen!"

My definition of the word "old" keeps changing. When I was in my 20s, I thought that 40 or 50 was old. Now that I'm in my 60s, I think of people in their 80s and 90s as old. So the number keeps moving up! It sounds simple, but there can be a lot of denial. And denial can be a comfortable friend, but only in the short term because eventually you do have to accept it.

I was raised in Europe until I was seven years old and that impacted heavily on my sensibilities about age. In some ways, people in Canada are more reserved. I don't know if my openness is just part of my character or if it's something I brought with me, having grown up in Europe. Certain things were not a big deal; no "putting an age on things" like the drinking age. You'd go to the corner pub when you were younger, and you'd get a drink with a little bit of beer and a bit of ginger ale. In Toronto, the drinking age used to be 21, and I got married when I was 19, so technically I wasn't allowed to drink at my wedding.

From my European culture I learned that it was alright to have wrinkles and that it's okay to start looking older, to have grey hair, to have white hair. In North American media, there's almost an expectation that if we're not going to do Botox or cosmetic surgery, we have to use fillers and more. I'm now hooked into this constant creaming of face and body. When I go to one of the major department stores and they tell me, "This is an anti-aging cream," I say, "Excuse me, there's no such thing, so let's talk about what's in these ingredients and what am I going to decide to buy." It's the language of advertising; it's so false that it's silly.

My dad was a high school teacher who taught math and machine shop, and held a chess club. He was forced to retire when he was 65. It was mandatory retirement and he did not cope well, he started to drink. He had a lot of capabilities and interests, but there was no preparation for retiring. He was totally depressed when he had to stop teaching. He did not talk much about retirement or what plans he had made or would make. He really tried; he was allowed to supply teach and that worked for a short time. He had a sister who lived in Spain, so he started to study Spanish, and then he had Italian neighbours, so he learned Italian. He tried to keep his brain active, but it wasn't enough.

My parents had a cottage, but as he drank more and became more ill, driving up to the cottage became too much for him. I remember that he was very upset when he was 80 years old and had to give up his driver's license. He didn't say too much about the driver's test, but he was angry. He said, "They've cut a part out of me." It was part of his manhood. But he would get too disoriented and confused to drive safely.

He said he was never an alcoholic, but if you really, really need to drink every day, to me you're an alcoholic. Because he was always drunk it was hard to tell that he had Alzheimer's. I knew nothing about Alzheimer's, and because he was also an alcoholic his deterioration was masked by the alcoholism. There was a point when my mom couldn't cope with his (what she thought was) alcoholism any more. So we put him in a hospice for a couple of weeks, and when he couldn't have anything to drink, we realized that something was really wrong. He wandered and was disoriented; he did not know where he was, so we ended up having to place him in a locked ward in a nursing home. I'm not sure when he first developed Alzheimer's, but he died when he was 86. This type of aging was a real eye-opener. My dad had been an intelligent, smart, vibrant person and had a very strong heart. Seeing that deterioration, seeing my dad change right in front of my eyes, was definitely traumatic for me.

My mother is quite stoic about aging. She'll say, "Oh, my knee hurts, but that's what happens when you get older," and she'll just continue on. She lives in a retirement residence now. I feel like I've been blessed with youthful DNA. My mom, who is 90, really does not look 90. She's friendly, smiling and walks straight, so I think that creates a more youthful appearance too.

I think some people want to be very old when they're still young. Possibly they are not happy with their personal lives, so there is no care about how they look. They say, "Who cares how I look." I'm starting to realize that some friends are aging well and some have given up working on looking the best they can, at any age. Sometimes when I'm at a meeting of peers, I can get a feel for how people think of themselves, when they don't care anymore about their appearance at all. As they age into their 50s, they give up, in a way. It takes too much effort to take care of themselves, and they don't have the energy or wherewithal to make it seem worthwhile.

My mother and I never had personal conversations. She didn't talk about going through mid-life, or my dad's retirement. We had conversations about my dad's drinking and their relationship, but we never discussed personal things about ourselves or shared our own personal transitions and difficulties. But I did not do that with any of my girlfriends either, and I'm not sure why. Maybe I was having a hard time with getting older and transitioning through menopause.

In some ways, I'm a very private person. I've kept to myself some of the things I'm going through because I want to process it and get through things myself. I don't want interference and criticism and judgment. There are times when I don't want to discuss or defend my position. Sometimes as life proceeds, the teachers come to you. For me that's come mostly from books. By flipping through the pages and involving myself in a book, I will find my answer to what I'm thinking about.

I feel that I'm a positive person and when some people phone me, I'm just drained afterwards. I think to myself, "You know what? I don't want to do that anymore." When I was younger, I had an endless flow of goodwill, but now I have to temper it because my energy is not unlimited. I'm stronger in being able to say what I want and not always pleasing those people who are not going to be positive peers and friends. I just had to stop some friendships.

Having a child was the most challenging experience in my life. It was, "Wow!" I had to learn patience and understanding. I had to learn that this baby was not developed to the point of having a discussion with me yet! I'd never done any babysitting, I had no brothers and sisters, I had no experience with young children — I had never held a baby! So it was huge. And there were no other children around us. I just sort of motored along. I was depressed, but I didn't really know it. I went back to work after six months, and I think that saved me from falling apart because I had to get it together to go to work. Later on I did go into therapy and that helped tremendously. You can read all the baby books and articles you want, watch programs and listen to podcasts, but I think until you actually physically go through it and feel your way through it, you can't predict everything ahead of time. I think I had to come to grips with the fear of a huge change.

The best thing about aging is living every stage of life as fully as possible, and trying not to limit myself. When someone asks me to do something, I'm already thinking of reasons not to and I'm learning to reverse that. So I said yes to my friend who invited me to a yoga ashram and that was living fully. I was truly living in the moment.

What I know about dying is what I've seen from my mother and father. I really don't want to have Alzheimer's like my dad — that would be horrendous. I don't want to be dying slowly for years and years. I hope that when I die, I'll be as sharp as a tack and in good shape until the moment it happens. There are people in my mother's retirement home, like her neighbour who celebrated her 101st birthday, and all they do is go for meals and sleep, eat and sleep. This is not a life to me. I fear dying more than death because I want it to be short and I don't know that it will be.

I think there is some commitment on my son's side, but I told him I certainly don't expect him to provide round-the-clock care, that's why there will be some money for someone to take care of me. When I talked with my son, he said to me, "Mom, please declutter!" So we're not talking about health or how to take care of me, he just says, "Please, please just get rid of some of this stuff. I don't want to have to go through it when you pass away!"

I hope I don't stay around too long if my mind is gone. The only preparation I can do is to make sure I have enough money so I can be in a place where I'm taken care of in a dignified way, and so I'm not suddenly a burden to someone else, and a vegetable. I don't see that happening, I don't have a vision of that happening to me.

I know my beliefs have evolved. I believe in reincarnation, in the white light, in a spirit world. I have always been an avid reader of New Age books, and many of the concepts of reincarnation and the afterlife resonate with me. I realized when I went on a recent yoga retreat that as I've gotten older, I've become more interested in the spiritual aspects of living. I've always said, even when I was a young woman, I do not believe in an organized church. I do believe in a type of spirit, God or whatever you want to call it, but I cannot pray to a god in that sense.

I've never had a fear of death because I feel that I'm going to live for a while, so I don't dwell on it. And part of the reason I don't fear it is I think it's another transition, that there is no real death. It's your soul transition. Maybe that's why it's not this huge concern for me. I'm more concerned about finding joy in life right now.

THE INVITATION

7

Lucy's Story

Lucy, 58 years old, grew up in Toronto and in the Near North. She dreams of living in British Columbia with all of her family. She feels most at home in nature. She works in health care as a massage therapist. She enjoys having dinner with friends and family, doing yoga and spending time with animals. Vintage jewellery, warm winter boots, meditation and music comfort her.

I imagine that Lucy and I are having this conversation on a sandy beach strewn with logs from the ocean. It is twilight and we are drinking hot lemon tea, laced with brandy. A campfire is roaring in front of us and the warm glow encloses us.

My parents died in their early 60s, so I don't feel like I really saw them in their older years; I don't know what aging parents are like, really. They died close together. My father died of lung cancer; my mother survived cancer, but died of a heart attack eight months after my father. It was a shock to me that my father died first because my mother had heart problems for as long as I can remember. It was also a shock because she went in for heart surgery and ended up dying.

    I was always close with my aunts, my mom's two older sisters, but became even closer to them after my mother died. I was especially close with one aunt, and she died soon after my parents. There's one piece of wisdom she gave me that I think of often. She told me, "I always figured anything after 70 (years old) was a bonus, but I'm getting tired of my bonuses." She died at age 75. That doesn't seem old now, but my aunt's doctor told her that she was a 110-pound woman who worked like a 180-pound man all her life. She was worn down.

I guess I saw a lot of ill health around me at an early age. Watching our parents struggle with their health, we each made very different choices. My brother, who is only six years older than me, developed adult onset diabetes in his early twenties. He did not try to control it with diet or exercise. His motto was always, "I am here for a good time, not a long time." I was 24 when I went into a career of nursing and saw so many sick people that I decided to try to be as healthy as I could. I felt that you're given a body, so you want to try to eat and do things to keep it vital and strong. I value my health and spend a lot of time and money on it.

There aren't a lot of benefits to aging in this culture. It's almost like there's an attempt to reverse it with skin cream or dyeing your hair. I think it's absolutely not true when they say that 60 is the new 40. I think that's crap, I really do. Our age is our age. There hasn't been a welcoming into aging. If anything, there's a whole lot of doom and gloom around it. When you look at the people who are our role models on television, most of them have had plastic surgery. That's a very different look, but they certainly don't look young. They look altered.

One person who has really influenced me is a friend of mine who is Aboriginal. My mother was part Aboriginal so there's a part of me that really connects to that. My friend had a ritual where she asked her close female friends to come together and celebrate her becoming an Elder. She's in this incredibly wonderful stage in her life and she's acknowledging that she's an older woman. She's very beautiful in many ways, so her spirit came through and also her honest attempt at wanting to make that journey in a meaningful, positive way.

The ritual was really beautiful. We began with a pipe ceremony.

She spoke of how she felt, how she wanted to come into this phase of her life in a good, honourable way. She explained that at one time, the transition to becoming an Elder was celebrated. She thanked her grandmothers (who are no longer with her) for all they had given her and asked them to help her to create a ceremony for her transition. They were her spirit guides. She also shared her thoughts on how things change, ceremonies change, life changes and how there's not a lot done to welcome people into the Elder role, so she wanted to create that.

Then everybody spoke. We spoke about our feelings towards her, our caring for her, and also what we thought of her becoming an Elder. I remember being moved by so many things that were said. There were several other women who were close to my age, in our mid-50s, but there were two fairly young women there, and what they said really resonated with me. They shared how much they love their grandmothers and their grandmothers' friends. One woman said the word for grandmother in her mother tongue is something like "kohkom," but they call them "Kukoos" because they are so cuckoo! They talked about how their grandmothers are such wonderful women who delight in seeing you as yourself. They are so accepting, so generous and are not trying to compete with you. They respected and trusted their grandmothers and felt they could go to them with their worries or their shame, and they weren't judged; they were accepted. Hearing how important older women were to these young women was incredibly moving. It was really healing for me to be part of that ritual, to acknowledge that we are growing old and moving into a different phase in life. It was about experiencing the joy of it.

I had an occasion when I realized how old I am! It was fairly early on a Saturday morning, I'd gone out to walk the dog and came back wet and muddy. I didn't have a shower yet because I was going out later, so I just put my pajamas and housecoat back on. Then I thought, "Oh, I have to vacuum." I'm at the point where I'm always losing my glasses and need them on to see while I'm vacuuming, so I thought I'd wear my prescription sunglasses. I had put egg white and honey on my face because it's supposed to be good for your skin. My son walked in and said, "Mom! What are you wearing?! Why are you wearing sunglasses?!" I realized how silly I looked, he just walked away laughing and I thought, "I wouldn't have done that as a young person!" So I felt like a "Kukoo"!

I'm about the same age as my close friends and we talk openly about aging. It's been invaluable for me to talk with them and have a group of friends growing older with me. We're changing; things change. We can all be kind of forgetful, slowing down a bit, realizing that things that were important aren't as important now. We're at the stage where it's not our parents getting ill, it's our peers who are getting ill. We're planning for a different part of our life now. It's reassuring to be able to talk to somebody openly and say, "You know, this part really sucks!" or, "This is kind of exciting!"

I remember my father saying to me, "Your mind doesn't change. You look in the mirror and you're surprised at how you look." I find that happening. I look in the mirror and see my face sagging and my neck wrinkling, and I think, "Oh my gosh, I don't look very good!" I really don't like the changes, but then I remember that when I was 20, I didn't like the way I looked either, so I try to accept who I am. If I had a choice, I'd rather look younger, but I really can't do anything about it.

I used to walk by men and they would look at me. And I don't get looked at anymore. I started to notice it when I was probably around 45. Because even when you're 40, 18-year-old guys will still check you out; you're still on their radar. Then I realized, hmm, I'm old.

When I look at young women now, I marvel at their beauty. I really hope they know how beautiful they are. I see them with their friends, with a look in their eyes that shows they don't look too confident. Also I notice how people need to be so made up today, with their nails, with their hair, with being waxed, looking almost perfect. That seems like such a hard thing today.

When I was younger I saw a lot of barriers. I thought I could not do a lot of things and did not have the confidence to even try. Not that I think I can do everything now, but at this point in my life I think that when I put my mind to something that is important to me, I can probably do it. It is also important to know when to give up doing the things I really can't do anymore, and to know the difference between the two.

So far I've been blessed that I haven't had any real physical ailments. I think that chronic illnesses are very difficult and people suffer a lot from them. I work in a profession where I see people with chronic illness, especially cancer. I think our will to live is so strong and I have seen the struggle of chronic illness. It is difficult when people are young, but they have youth on their side and a relatively strong body. When you see chronic illness in older people, they want to live, but sometimes every step is a drain. I think that's really hard.

My death doesn't scare me too much. My husband, yes, I fear his death and living alone. I definitely fear dying more than death. Some of the ways of dying are pretty frightening. The idea of not breathing — our instinct to survive is so strong that even if we don't breathe for a little bit of time, if we're choking or coughing, it's a very, very alarming feeling. Even if you try to be calm, it's scary. So yes, it will be a terrifying thing, that passage. It's the going on and on in that half-life until you die that frightens me. And I think it's hard to leave. I think it's hard to die. It's hard to choose death. I'm not talking about it like I want to commit suicide. I don't mean that at all. I hope I don't keep trying to prolong something that's inevitable, that I have the wisdom to say, "Enough is enough. I don't want more treatment for this." I think that's a very difficult thing to do because we're so adaptable as humans. We can think, "Oh, I could never live like this," but we can. Often the changes are insidious, we live with them and adapt. Unfortunately with modern medicine the way it is, we can prolong and prolong, and I don't believe in that. I hope I have the courage and strength to remember that when the time comes.

8

Ruth's Thoughts on Dying: How I Became An Amazonian

I learned the most about dying from my dad. He told me repeatedly, "I'm living on borrowed time."

My dad had clocks and timepieces and calendars and datebooks everywhere. Everywhere. He had a dresser drawer filled with boxes of watches. In his home office, he had a wall calendar and a desk calendar, a clock on the wall and a desk clock. He was acutely aware of time and grateful for every second he lived. He had almost died, many times.

As a child with multiple ear infections, he had so many surgeries that the surgeon became his buddy and arranged to have the same room for him, Room no. 1. This was in the 1920s, when the risk of infection was high, and there were times he experienced dangerously high fevers. His good-luck blankie and his mom comforted him back to health.

When he was 20 years old, he was interned in the Flossenbürg and Dachau concentration camps during the Holocaust. He was starved, beaten, and exhausted. He required surgery for an infection in his right leg, from trying to use wire to keep his disintegrating boots together. There was no anesthetic, of course.

As a soldier in his 20s, he battled to establish the state of Israel. There were many skirmishes and battles — among them was one in particular when a bomb landed, hit his troop and killed several men. He was the only one who escaped unharmed.

When he was 33 years old and studying for his PhD degree, he was riding his motorbike and a truck drove into him. He said he could see his foot by his shoulder. He went into a coma, and contracted pneumonia, followed by a fat embolism. He survived it all. The surgeon told him that to kill him one would need to drop him from an airplane without a parachute. His doctor wrote up my Dad's rare medical situation into a case study that landed him in a journal of medicine.

When I was 19, I worked in a jewellery store, and with my first paycheque I bought my dad a watch. It was probably a bit too shiny and too gold for his taste, but he wore it proudly at important occasions and celebrations for the rest of his years. One day, not long after I gave him the watch, he told me he felt he was living on borrowed time, that he should have died many times over for all the near-catastrophes and almost fatal circumstances he'd survived. It was his mental strength and fierce will to live that kept him going. Each time he healed himself back to life.

With the passing years, he surrounded himself with more and more clocks and calendars, daily reminders of the preciousness of life and how exquisitely full the days are with time.

I had no idea what kind of damage these traumatic experiences had on his brain, so it was both unsurprising and shocking to me that he developed memory loss in his 80s. He was still operating his business, but having difficulty doing things that he had done for decades: trouble-shooting computer and lab instrument issues, providing consultations to professionals, and completing routine tasks.

We talked about whether he should go through a neurological assessment. It would mean meeting with a team including a geriatrician, registered nurse, social worker, and perhaps an occupational therapist, to be assessed for several hours with a battery of tests, questionnaires and interviews. There would be six-month follow-up appointments from then onwards to monitor the progression of the neurological illness. I believed that receiving a diagnosis of dementia would be more harmful than helpful for my dad's well-being. Each follow-up assessment would be an exercise in stress, anxiety and humiliation for my parents, and there was no known treatment that would cure it. They were already doing everything possible with their lifestyle to slow it down. My dad, mom and I could tell whether the illness had progressed functionally anyway, better than more cognitive testing.

Working in health care helped me understand how to approach the medical environment. I learned that the focus in medicine is on assessing, diagnosing and treating, on helping people live and not die. I knew when to ask questions and what questions to ask. I respected the health care professionals, the nurses and doctors, for their medical expertise, but knew that they were not experts on my dad. They needed us, the family, to be available to help them, and we needed them, too.

He wasn't always the best dad. We didn't always have the best relationship. Some years we were closer, others we were far apart. When I was little, I looked up to him — tall, handsome, smart, blue eyes, and kind with a gentle smile. I drew him a picture every day and when he returned home from work, I ran to show him and was greeted with his joy. We watched television together, me curled up in his lap or beside him, holding hands, enjoying *Bonanza, Hogan's Heroes, M*A*S*H*, the typical 70s television shows that six-year-old girls watched.

I felt my dad in my life: weekend outings to buy groceries and my dad tearing huge bites out of Hungarian salami sandwiches on crusty rolls, not caring about the crumbs on the seats; swimming and canoeing together on summer weekends; driving me to figure skating classes; driving me to ballet classes, which my dad loved because he could watch the hips of my ballet teacher. We may have as many photos of Miss Doris and her hips, as we do of me dancing ballet.

Then, when I was 12, he disappeared into a massive career change. He was in his 50s, and decided to leave his job at the hospital to start a laboratory for hair analysis and nutritional evaluation. Our house was sold, he moved from Montreal to Toronto to launch his business, and my mom and I moved into a flat in Montreal, where she continued to work and support the family.

That separation was difficult and painful for me. My dad was birthing his new work baby, and his focus, energy and time were spent labouring on this new enterprise. Sometimes it seemed to the 12-year-old me that he loved his new business more than his daughter. I missed him terribly. We saw each other during monthly visits, but I felt like I had lost my dad.

A couple of years later we reunited in a Toronto suburb. I was a full-on moody, messy 14-year old starting a high school in a new town and that did not make things easier for our relationship. I had no idea who my father was now, there was a blur of passing one another, each of us going through our own identity crisis.

When I was in university, we began to have interesting conversations about political and social issues, but it wasn't until I started to work full-time and live on my own that we really connected as adults. We both wanted to improve our relationship, and my dad reached out and invited me for lunch. We left our respective work places, drove halfway and enjoyed a meal together, just the two of us. It was usually a Chinese food restaurant with buffet lunch: won ton soup, chicken chow mein, spicy beef with string beans, pots of jasmine tea and a fortune cookie. These father-daughter lunch dates were memorable. He talked about how hard it was for him, for his ego, to put himself out there and promote his new business, in his third language. I talked about what it was like to be a clinician in the health care system, what I was learning about getting older and that I was going to make sure I took care of my health as best I could. Those moments alone in conversation taught me who my father was as a man, as an entrepreneur, as an elder, and as a friend, and he discovered who I was as a young adult and his grown daughter. Our relationship continued to deepen as we aged, and I valued it more with every year lived.

≥●

For five years, the cognitive deterioration continued and my dad went from having a mild cognitive impairment (MCI) to moderate cognitive loss. I supported my mom so she could support my dad. The three of us went grocery shopping, ran errands and dined out altogether. I accompanied my mom to the opera instead of my dad (to his great joy). As stressful and sad as these times were for our family, they were special, too. I learned what tender loving care meant down to its tiniest details: my mom brought my dad breakfast in bed, including oatmeal or toast, his green supplements drink and medications, and she took care of messes quietly and respectfully. She focused on the love, always the love.

My dad became physically and cognitively frail, and even though he relied on me more, I did not experience role reversal. I never became his parent and he never became a child. He was still my parent, albeit my ill parent. I was giving more physical support for sure, but he was giving too, emotionally and spiritually. His sense of organization, judgment and comprehension were slowly deteriorating, but he was still competent. If there was a decision to be made, we discussed it. Respect was an important value to both of us and I felt that we were partners in his care. We had the moments of deep intimacy and vulnerability that often surface in an illness: like sitting side-by-side, holding hands while we watched television, when he felt too unwell to do anything else.

A couple of months before he died my dad had a small stroke. It resolved quickly, but he was hospitalized for monitoring and to adjust his medications. There were some issues that resulted from the stroke: his speech was slightly slurred, his word-finding difficulty worsened and he was more fatigued.

We were sitting on a bench together outside the hospital, enjoying the May sunshine. I thought this was a good time to have an important conversation, here at the hospital where life-and-death happened every moment.

As we watched people walk by, I asked my dad, "Are you scared?"

"Of what?"

"Of anything?"

"Death?"

"Yes, that too."

Dad shrugged his shoulder, waved his hand, and shook his head, "No."

I wanted to ask him more. I wanted his guidance. I also wanted him to know that I was okay to talk about him dying.

So I asked, "How do you want to die? I'll give you four options: stroke, heart attack, cancer, or infection. What would be your preference?"

My dad was quiet as he thought. Then he replied, "It does not matter. You are smart."

So it did not matter to him how he died. He was comfortable with whatever way death would happen for him. I don't know that I was smart, but I was feeling connected with him as we held hands during this big conversation.

A month later, my dad was back in the hospital, he actually walked into the emergency department. He could not urinate. He was diagnosed with a urinary tract obstruction and they tried to catheterize him, but the blockage was too large and they were unsuccessful. He was admitted because not urinating can lead to sepsis and death. The next day, the urologist came to discuss the situation and offered us options, primarily surgical.

I asked, "Do you want a procedure to have a catheter inserted or have surgery to remove the blockage?"

"No. I want them to leave me alone," he replied.

My dad understood that if the blockage were not removed, if he could not urinate, then he would eventually die. He had been open and vocal about his wish to die with dignity, wanting no heroic measures, no invasive procedures and to be treated with respect and kindness. Years earlier he wrote a letter addressed to me with his Advanced Directives, understanding the deep responsibility that went along with it. When it came to this moment, to make this treatment decision, I remembered the family conversations about dying and death.

The decision about whether to do the surgery was difficult. It was layered with his wishes and his values. It involved his level of readiness: had he squeezed all the juice out of this life he loved so much? It was likely that his cognition would worsen with the anesthesia and his quality of life would deteriorate too.

We didn't go ahead with the surgical procedure.

I showed the urologist the letter of my dad's advanced directives. He read it and asked us, "So, you want no active treatment, only comfort measures?"

We replied, "Yes."

Making that treatment decision hung in the shadows of his gloomy ward room — unspoken and unacknowledged. Nursing staff referred to us as the family members who refused the surgery. I wondered what the health care staff treating my dad believed about dying and death. What happened for them when their parent was dying? What treatment decisions did they make?

One day while he was being "freshened up," he yelled so loudly that I could hear it down the hallway. He swore loudly in Hungarian, the language of colourful curses. There were two personal care workers there with my mother. I was upset, distraught to hear his distress.

I walked into the hospital room and said, "Enough, enough. I have never heard my father curse so loudly that I could hear it from down a hallway. Why was he yelling?"

My dad said to the staff, "Don't be so rough. I am a human being."

Then my dad turned to look at me and said, "You have to protect me."

My heart split open and I realized that this was a turning point. There was no going back. I had to assert myself in order to advocate for him.

We requested that my dad be moved to the palliative care unit. One of the palliative physicians came to speak with my dad, my mom and me, to find out what our wishes were and whether we were comfortable with the protocols of palliative care: minimal monitoring and minimal medications, other than pain management. Yes, yes we were.

I did not yet know that we were creating an opportunity to have our final conversations together, and for my parents to say goodbye to each other.

When my dad realized he was going to die, something amazing happened. His slurred speech improved, his word finding improved, and his lethargy disappeared. I wondered, "What happened to his cognitive impairment?" He spoke clearly in full sentences, and engaged in loving and meaningful conversations with us.

But how was this possible? I'd never read or heard of this before. Had he willed himself to be present to talk with us? It felt like a miracle happened.

Months later, after my father died, I asked a friend who was a former speech language pathologist. She said that there was no scientific research or scientific reason that she was aware of that might explain his improvement or his clarity. She wondered whether it was possible that his brain had re-organized itself with the power of his love for us.

The palliative care staff taught me about the final stages of dying. I was humbled and shocked to realize that I had no knowledge or awareness of the dying process. I was not taught it — not at home, not at school, not in university, not in my work in geriatric health care. I was taught how human beings are conceived and born, but hardly anything about how we die, and death.

My earliest education about death was when I was about eight years old. My 17-year-old brother was babysitting me. We were hanging out and I asked him, " What will happen to mom and dad when they die? How do people die?"

My brother said, "I'm not telling you because you're going to cry."

I begged him, "Please, please! I promise I won't cry!"

After going back and forth for a while, my brother asked, "You promise?"

I nodded.

My brother said, "Okay. It's when their hearts stop beating. We die when our heart stops beating."

I started to sob.

My brother said, "You promised!"

"I know. I'm sorry. Is that how? Our hearts stop beating and we die?"

I remember how shocking it sounded, the suddenness and the finality of it. One moment alive; the next moment dead.

My dad needed my mom and me to be there with him. I cleared everything from my life to be available. We were there to advocate for him, to comfort him so that he could relax and have energy to do the work of letting go and releasing himself to die.

My dad spoke to us about his dying. He told us he felt it.

I asked, "How do you know you're dying?"

"I have no energy."

"How do you know that you are not just sick and will get better, but that you are dying?"

"The doctors have given up on me," he said.

I asked, "How are you feeling, are you in pain?"

"Dying is not fun," he replied.

"You are leading the way. It's up to you."

"The direction is not good," he said.

We felt deep pain, sadness and shock knowing that he was dying from our lives. I think dying is hard to do. I imagine having to let go of life, of all the people you love, of the hope that you will have another day to live — letting go of all that and going into the unknown.

My dad's dying room in the palliative care unit felt like a love nest, filled with affection, warmth and gratitude. My brother flew in to spend time alone with dad and to be together as a family; those moments were deeply memorable and poignant. It was the last time the four of us would be together.

My dad said, "It's not good to die. Such a loving family. Pity to leave it. Dying is not a pleasure. There is no continuation. I am saddened to leave you. It's hard to leave such a loving atmosphere. I am surrounded by love."

It was around this time that I realized how grateful I felt to the interviewees and for our conversations. I remembered their stories, their courage and how they faced their fears or didn't, how willing they were to talk about what helped, and what still hurts them today. I felt supported and inspired by them.

A couple of weeks before my dad died, he exclaimed as he came out of a deep sleep, "Oh, so delicious! Oh so good!"

My mom and I looked at each other with incredulity. She asked him, "What? What is delicious? What is good?"

He didn't reply. I wondered. He seemed to be in a state of high gratitude.

With each passing day my dad grew weaker. One afternoon my mom asked him, "Do you want to sleep?"

He said, "No. It's a shame to waste this time. Soon, I'll sleep a lot."

His pain scared me. Seeing my dad suffer was the worst. I asked him if he felt pain and watched closely for any signs. There were times that he grimaced, grinded his teeth, groaned, shouted and flailed his arms. Most of it was involuntary, and it was distressing for me and my mom to watch. Despite all my education and training, I didn't know that agitation was part of dying, especially possible for someone with a cognitive impairment. How did I not know this given my career in geriatric health care?

There were nurses who were so gentle and kind that my dad did not utter a sound other than a stream of thank-yous. We discovered that not everyone provided that level of care and they knew this amongst themselves. As one woman told us, "Not every nurse is an angel."

We spoke with the medical doctor and the nurses in charge of his care. It took a team effort to manage his pain — my mom, myself and the health care team — and we tried different ways: the massage therapist taught us how to massage his feet and calves, nurses placed pillows underneath his swollen legs to keep him comfortable and prevent skin breakdown, we held his hand, my mom stayed when staff "freshened him up," we played his favourite music, and we listened for what he wanted to share with us in the moment.

One nurse, Miryam, was incredible. She told us that she noticed my dad had declined greatly in the week since she had first seen him.

He was in so much pain by then that it took three nursing staff plus my mom to help when they needed to move him. He was no longer able to turn and he cried out, but he understood Miryam when she told him she was going to take his blood pressure and responded to her by extending his arm. He had had his own blood pressure kit at home and loved monitoring it himself. Miryam talked to us about increasing his pain medications, and she contacted the physician to request increasing the quantity and the frequency. Sleep, Dad. Sleep

I knew he would die that Sunday. I sensed it from his breathing. I sensed it from how peaceful he was, how beautiful he looked a couple of days earlier. I sensed it from how he had looked at us with such love in his eyes, the fullness of love he felt. He looked at my mom; they looked at each other with that same look I had seen in photos from 60 years ago. He was ready to die and he was letting us know that this was it; he was slipping into the deep sleep.

That Sunday in July was full of weather. There were rainstorms brewing with dark charcoal grey clouds, on and off rain. It felt like a gloomy day in summer that was readying to welcome a dying soul.

He knew, he was aware the whole time, sleeping deeply, but not unconscious or in a coma, occasionally waking so that we could connect with our eyes. I could touch him, hold his hand, kiss his cheek, whisper, "Dad, I love you." Sometimes he vocalized back to me; sometimes he was quiet.

Many people asked me afterwards if we were there with him when he died. He never asked us to be there with him and I never asked him if he wanted that. I suppose it was not a concern for me. He was not scared

of death, he liked his own company and did not mention wanting someone with him.

We weren't there. I am quite sure that was deliberate on my dad's part. He chose to die the moment we left. He was not fearful or anxious, he felt comfortable, loved, and at peace. He knew that his wife (my mom) did not want to be there, that the pain would overwhelm her. When we kissed him that final good night, I can imagine him thinking, "Oh, they are going. Now I can go, too."

It feels strange and weird to say this as a non-believer so here it goes: I felt reborn. My dad's death was a peak experience of loving energy. I learned to see death through the lens of love.

9

David's Story

David is an 84-year-old husband, and father of seven children. Years ago, one of his daughters was killed in a car accident. He was born in Montreal, moved to Toronto in the '60s. David worked in sales and as a manufacturers' agent, as a philanthropist and fundraiser. He loves skiing, travelling, painting and spending time with his family at their cottage.

When David is sharing his thoughts with me, I feel as though we are sitting together in the rooftop garden of a high-rise, nestled into cushioned armchairs, sipping iced tea on a warm, clear day.

There's a part of me that's comfortable with dying and there's a part of me that wants to live.

When I was in my teenage years, about 17, I was very, very sick. Everything was wrong with me: I had double vision, my kidney was shot, everything was shot, I couldn't do anything. I wasn't even allowed to listen to the radio. I was unconscious for about ten days and there was little likelihood that I would survive. It was then that I saw the tunnel of light.

The other day I was at a book club and a woman was talking about death and birth. I think she was sharing her answer to the question, "What was your first thought?" She described how she envisioned a child being born, as it comes down the tunnel (so to speak), and all of a sudden it sees daylight for the first time. It gave me a weird feeling because that was the feeling I had when I was 17 years old and in that tunnel myself; I saw the light at the end of the tunnel. I wondered, "Am I being reborn?"

The doctor who was treating me said, "David, the only way you'll survive is if you have something to look forward to each day and every day." It was the best advice I ever had because from then on, no matter what, I made up my mind that I would always look forward to something. I'm a real fighter. I have to stay alive: for my children or for my wife or to finish my life story or a painting I still have to do. I promised my wife that I'd stay around, although she might want to change her mind! I don't want to let my family down. It's been my motto, that's what I always preach to people. It's engrained in my subconscious. People say live in the present, but the future was always exciting to me. So even today when I think of death, for example, I think, "Oh, that sounds kind of exciting!"

I retired when I was 60 because the fun had gone out of business and at the time I had two very young children, 8 and 6 years old. The fact that my wife was a doctor who earned a very good income helped. I retired to be a good father and look after my children. I soon discovered if you're a busy person during your working career, you'll be busy in retirement.

When I retired I ended up doing a lot of volunteer work. I was involved with several different charities. I got involved in one of my children's schools as a chairman of their charity. This child is handicapped, has learning disabilities and went to a special school. I'd never thought of being a fundraiser, but I turned out to be fairly successful at raising funds. Then I became president of another charity that opened up a summer camp for children under 12 with disabilities, and raised a lot of money to get the camp off the ground. I resigned from that and then had a heart attack. I was 66 years old. I think my heart attack was probably due to running these charities! That was very difficult — having a heart attack — and what helped me was going to the Cardiac Rehab Centre. It gave me a sense of purpose and helped me with the transition.

After I had my heart attack, I felt that I'd paid my debt to society and I stopped volunteering with charities. I ventured into many activities I'd never done during my business career, like acrylic painting, skiing, golf, Toastmasters (public speaking), computer courses, improvisation and travelling. I think of growing old as an opportunity, so I really enjoy it.

The frustrating thing with getting old is that your mind stays young, but you know you can't do the things you used to do. We have a year-round cottage and when we bought it, my wife and I were very active in fixing it up. We loved it. We'd go up with the family every weekend and work on it. That's not true anymore and I miss that. I skied up until I was 72. It got to the point that I wasn't enjoying skiing because I was frightened that I would have another heart attack and I didn't want another one! So I had to give up skiing. I'm grateful that I've been able to replace what I had to give up with positive, enjoyable activities.

I used to tell people that I was ten years older than I was and they'd tell me how great I looked for my age. I reached the point — 80 was the magic number — when I told people my age. I don't know why 80. It just seemed like a great number. In my mind I thought that if I could live to 80, it would be quite the accomplishment. It seemed you could say you are old when you're 80, and if you could have a youthful approach to life when you're 80, so much the better.

When I was a young person, I was a very cocky, conceited individual. I wasn't a nice person. I'm a much better, more well-rounded person now, even though I can't do all the things I used to. I don't think I'm an A-type person anymore. I'm much calmer and more considerate, I guess, of other people. I've matured enough to live a fairly good philosophy in life. Each day I try to achieve something because I find that by achieving something I'm keeping myself happy. I also try to do a good deed. Now I think in terms of making people smile, more than

DAVID'S STORY

anything. If I haven't made someone laugh or smile during the day, then I haven't been a success.

Lately I've been giving a lot of thought to my three marriages. I've been married 63 years of my entire life. Apparently, I love marriage! I've been reviewing my life in order to help my children, because a lot of things that I've experienced will tell the children about the pitfalls and opportunities that were created for me and for them.

I was first married at 22 and fell madly in love with this glamorous woman — everybody mistook her for Elizabeth Taylor, so that gives you an idea of how glamorous she was. Unbeknownst to me her one thought was "riches," so while I buried myself in work she apparently played around. I was warned by a friend of mine, who had gone to school with her, that she was very promiscuous, and I didn't believe him because I was so madly in love with her. We were married for 17 years and we had three children together. My daughter died when she was 16 years old. That had an impact on my life. We got divorced after 17 years of marriage, and that was after both my daughter and my father had died.

Then I went into a tailspin and met my second wife. I was about 39 when I met her, so it was definitely a rebound situation. And how I met her was a funny experience. We were on the train from Toronto to Montreal and she was sitting across from me with her boyfriend. There used to be a bar car on the old Montreal train and it was a boxcar converted into a nightclub. So what happened this night, the train left at 4 o'clock and was supposed to arrive in Montreal at 9 o'clock at night. We didn't get in until five o'clock in the morning because there was a derailment, and I ended up being invited on a ski trip with her boyfriend! So we had a ball in that bar car! She and I got along famously well. She was a model and we drank the bar car dry until it closed. It was a trip to remember, but it was a very expensive trip for me because I ended up getting married and divorced very quickly, and had to make another settlement! I knew at the time that we got married that it was a bad thing to do. I had a horrible honeymoon. That's another story.

I went into a self-destructive mode. I quit my job. My father had died, my daughter had been killed and I lost my motivation. I became a bum, literally a bum — I mean I slept on the streets, asked for cigarette money. It was a horrible feeling and I was aware of the fact that everything I was doing was wrong. Basically what happened was I'd lost all my confidence.

One day I had a dream — I was in this pit and somehow I got out of it but I didn't get out of it the normal way, it was some backward way. That gave me encouragement. In hindsight, it probably gave me my philosophy that when things are going well, start worrying because things are going to get a whole lot worse, and when things are bad, rejoice because it's going to get better.

It was a real struggle, a very gradual, uphill battle. I went through a number of different jobs, became a heavy drinker, and then I met my third wife, Judy. My second wife knew Judy's husband very well so that's how we met. We were invited to the same social events, and so on and so forth. When my daughter died, there's a picture of me with my head on Judy's shoulder falling asleep on the flight to my daughter's funeral. I knew right then and there that Judy was the right person for me and it's been proved right. We've been married going on 40 years.

It was only after marrying Judy, and after I started to give back, that I turned my life around. Judy had said, "If you're going to drink, that's it!" The best thing that happened was that I decided to go to an alcohol rehab centre. I had been an alcoholic up to that point in time. I should give you a description of what an alcoholic is — it is not the amount of liquor you consume, it's when liquor starts to cause problems. You can have one drink and it can cause you problems. And liquor was causing me a lot of problems! Something happened in rehab and I don't know what it was, but it changed my whole life. To this day, I still try to figure out what it was that actually changed because since then, I never wanted to have another drink and that was 20-odd years ago. I started to do very positive things again and the more positive things I did, the better I felt and the more my self-esteem increased. I began to revert back to my childhood self, which was entirely different from the person during this depressed period. I had been a fun-loving kid, I could make people laugh and I enjoyed making people laugh. People had thought of me as the comedian. So that all began to re-emerge and it continues to grow.

I read a book by Emerson, his Essay on Compensation, which was the most impactful book I'd read in my life. Basically it said that life is but a balance of good and bad. So you could translate that the more horrifying an experience you've had, the more glorious the good times will be. I've thought of that constantly and I've had some horrible experiences in life, but I've had some fabulous experiences that created great joy.

When I reached 80, my body started to really disintegrate. Your health deteriorates as you get older and you have to expect that — you don't have the body of an 18-year-old. You're going to have aches and pains. I have felt old probably when I've been in severe pain. When it is continuous, it can be depressing and it does affect me mentally to the point where I wonder if life is worth it. The feeling of helplessness takes over and I basically can't do anything. I get weaker, especially after going into hospital, because every time I come out I'm basically weaker than when I went in. I've been in the hospital so many times.

Then a few years ago I started on dialysis, which limits me. I think the biggest thing that happened to me was I couldn't travel anymore. That had a really negative impact on my life because I had to think of something else to look forward to, so my painting helped me to carry on. And since then my falls have helped me to carry on, I can look forward to falling! I did get a fear of falling, at one point I was terrified of it, but now it doesn't bother me. I fall very gently. I've finessed the technique so I do limited damage to myself, although I've had some funny falls and every fall is different. The time I did the most damage was when I still had macular degeneration, and that particular day they had stuck needles in my eyes, so I couldn't see where I was walking.

I went into a couple of comas and at one point they couldn't wake me up. They called my wife to get to the hospital right away because I was on the threshold. And I was very comfortable. I was in a beautiful dream and I was at peace. It was so comfortable. Yeah. The doctors were pounding on my chest trying to get me to wake, and then my youngest daughter came in and she said, "Dad!" And I woke up! When I did wake up, I felt at peace and I haven't had a worry since then. If it wasn't for Judy and the children, I'd have no quality of life — they've been tremendous.

I've done everything but die. I could sulk because I'm pretty immobilized and have to do dialysis four times a day, day in, day out. I never have a break. I was told last year that I have a year to live. So, what the hell, there's a dance in the old man yet!

Life is what I make of it. I've had a wonderful life. I've had many sad days, but life's been good to me. The part that is scary about death is leaving the family, saying goodbye. I worry about them. I worry about all my children. I worry about my wife. But I know, I worry too much. It's not only a matter of quality versus quantity of life. It's also another equation: do you still feel that you have more to give? Once I feel I have no more to give, I will be ready to die.

David died in October 2016 at the age of 86. Months earlier, I visited him in the hospital and read his story aloud to him. He gave his approval and said he was grateful that it would be published. We exchanged an embracing hug in silent recognition. During his Celebration of Life, David's family shared stories filled with his humour-filled wisdom. His youngest daughter, Courtney, is the next storied interview.

≈

10

Courtney's Story

Courtney is 30 years old biologically, but often feels 10 years older. Her career portfolio includes Senior Resident Anthropologist in an innovation design firm, research strategist at an insights firm, children's ski coach and Yin/Vinyasa yoga instructor. She is currently studying energy medicine and shamanic studies. Courtney loves dancing to fun music, wearing fun blazers and colourful scarves, and spending time with her dogs, Trapper and Hobbit. She is also David's daughter.

The conversation with Courtney feels like it's happening after dark. We are sitting at a booth in a smoky jazz lounge and the soulful music wafts in and out of her story.

One of the most challenging transitions in my life was right after university. From the time I was four years old until I was 24, I was in school and a student. I knew how to do that really well. After that, what was I going to do? I didn't know where to start, and you're not really taught what to do after academia. This transition was about the change in my identity and becoming an independent adult. I was faced with many decisions and the reality of aging parents.

Around that time, I met a spiritual mentor who helped me, and I learned to be okay with the unknown, to go with the flow and not grip so tightly to figure things out or control things. Regardless of all the times I've been anxious, nothing has ever been a disaster. Everything has led me to where I am, so now when I get nervous about not knowing what's next I just think, "Well, I've been here before and it's always worked out." As long as I keep my focus on the life I want to live and how I am meant to give back to the world, I don't worry about everything. There's a constant cycle of re-birthing and opening up to new opportunities. It can be scary at times, but I have a greater sense of trust that the universe or Spirit has a way of working everything out.

It's exciting to get older, at least that's what I feel now, being 30. It's an opportunity to continue growing, exploring what I like and what I don't like. The way I look at it is that I don't know how the next year will unfold, so aging is a really mysterious process; I see it as an evolution of self. I'm an optimistic person, so it just keeps getting better with every year that goes by. I gain more knowledge, experience and clarity about what I'm here to do and what I want to get out of life. There's something great about every age, although there will always be a part of me that feels, "Oh, I loved when I was that age." I believe that we walk with our previous selves still inside, that they are still a part of us that can surface in a given moment.

My parents have taught me a lot about aging and how to turn aging on its head. They are busting stereotypes about what it means to get older for their generation. My dad is in his 80s, and up until a few years ago, he was really active, travelling around the world with my mom, doing improv, still skiing, still very sharp and involved in my and my sisters' lives. My mom is in her late 60s, and she still does ballet classes and goes horseback riding. They've shown me that just because you reach a certain age, it doesn't mean that it will shape how you feel or what you can and can't do. I've never seen my parents accept what other people say is normal for when you're old. They had my sister and me later in life, so they've shown me that you don't have to rush into things because you won't be able to do them later. So I have my parents who are older and act one way, and then there are all these stereotypes and images of what it means to be old in the media that are very different.

Over the last few years, my dad has become more physically frail. He has been admitted into the hospital several times. While we have dealt with his health issues most of my life — he had his first heart attack when I was 12, and later diabetes, kidney disease and other issues — in 2012 things changed more drastically. My mom and I were away at a mother-daughter art retreat one weekend in September. We both felt nervous about going away because my dad seemed weaker than usual. Then on the Sunday we received a phone call telling us that my dad had decided to take himself to the hospital because he wasn't feeling well. I don't remember what the cause was that time; he's been in the hospital so many times since then.

My mom is a doctor, and I always felt safe knowing that she would be able to take care of and "fix" my father. I always had a sense that despite any physical illness, the combination of my dad's will to live and my mom's medical expertise would keep him alive no matter what. For me, what was the scariest part in that moment when we got the call was that my mom started to cry. It was one of the few times in my entire life where I have seen my mom cry. I knew it was serious. I remember she got up and walked out of the art studio. I knew — I felt that something was wrong, so I followed her out and around the corner where I saw her crying. I remember sensing that she felt embarrassed about it, that she was ashamed. My heart hurt witnessing her tears. I wanted to cry just seeing her cry. It is rare to see her express vulnerability or fear; she's an incredible woman who is always taking care of so many people, including my sister with special needs. In that moment, I gave her a hug and didn't say anything. It was a very quick interaction, but it stayed with me. It was a shift for me, from her being a pillar of strength all the time to seeing her being real, feeling painful emotion. I'm glad she did — I don't want her to hold things in and try to pretend that everything's okay. For me, it was a wake-up call that death is real no matter how well or hard you try to mask it.

COURTNEY'S STORY

My dad was very weak, so when he was discharged he went to stay for a while at a retirement home to receive care. Based on that, my mom decided to sell the house. I just remember her saying she was going to sell the house and before I knew it, it was on the market and was sold. That was my childhood home; I had never lived anywhere else. That winter we purged everything. My dad was back home, but still not doing great. At the same time, I ended a three-year relationship and changed jobs. It was an emotionally tumultuous time, with a lot of uncertainty.

Over the past couple of years I've been anticipating my dad's death; I've grieved so much and gone through many moments of deep sadness and crying. I felt a shift this past year when he was in the hospital. I've done so much looking at my relationship with my dad, my attachment to him and letting it go, that I'm at the point now where yes, I'll be extremely sad and it's going to be hard, but I also feel that he's holding on when his quality of life is so terrible. There's so much stress I sometimes wonder, "Why is this happening again? Why does he need to hold on? We're going to be fine." It's going to be hard no matter when it happens. Now it's about whether he can do one more operation or whether to get him a nurse, and it goes on and on. How long can that go on?

I haven't had that conversation with him. I have these conversations with other people like my half-sister (my dad's daughter from his second marriage), but I find it very difficult to have it with my dad or my mom. I don't know if he's ready to admit that he's ready to go. I think it's hard because I think he's scared. He puts on a pretty good show, but I think he's actually scared of it coming. In the hospital I've said to him at times, "I'll be okay, the family is going to be okay and I support you in whatever you need or want to do."

It's not a common topic to be talking about, "Oh, let's talk about your death." I probably could, it just seems awkward and out of the blue. I don't know when I would do it, or where I would do it or what I would say, like, "Hey, I've been thinking about your death, and how you're doing." I have had the opportunity when I'm with him in the hospital; it's in front of me. How do I gracefully bring up the topic of his impending death? I have no idea when I say goodbye to him in the evening what's going to happen, so every moment, every word that we exchange together counts.

Understandably, my dad very much steers the conversation away from himself. Because he's in so much pain a lot of the time, he doesn't want to talk about it or his health issues. He goes straight to, "And how are you doing? Tell me about your life and your work." I think he doesn't like to talk to me about feeling sad, scared or depressed. He feels that he needs to be strong and protect his children from pain. To have more open, honest conversations with him is something that is definitely on my mind, and something that I think we need more of in life. It never seems like the right time to talk about death.

My dad's experience has made me realize that I don't want to go in and out of the hospital when I am older. I know that every time he's gone in to the hospital he comes out that much weaker, that much more depressed and often it hasn't been totally necessary. With my dad, it hasn't been a very graceful process. I feel that he's still holding on, thinking that he has to protect us or be there for us. But if I get to that point, I want to do what's right for me — mentally, energetically, emotionally — realize that it's my time. I hope that my death is more seamless with less of these ups and downs, and that it happens more quietly and easily.

I honour that dying is something that's really important, rather than the end of something that I forget about and throw away. It's about helping the dying person into their next stage although we don't know what that is, we don't know what's going to come. It's a mystery. I think we could be better at honouring and respecting a dying person. They should be surrounded by people who love them, like it's something to be celebrated. That feels better to me than someone being apart from their family. In the institutional hospital setting that's more difficult, people are being looked after by strangers and all these pieces of equipment and medicine that alters how their body naturally wants to be.

When I think about my own death, I'd like it if I could die having the support of friends and family around me. I'd love for it to be a celebration of my life, and I want people to share memories of me and stories of my life. I'd love to be in a comfortable, beautiful space, somewhere that's peaceful and calming. I would like it to be a graceful, easy transition. I wish that for my dad as well.

THE INVITATION

❧

11

Sylvia's Story

Sylvia is a 70-year-old woman who feels that she is in her wisdom years. She has a triple-major arts degree — English, history and anthropology. She married young, had three children, divorced in her late 30s, and raised these special souls to be full participants in the world community. Professionally Sylvia was a private English tutor, a teacher of English as a Second Language, a researcher/writer for CBC documentaries, and an award winning technical writer. She has worked as an organizational development consultant and executive coach in both the private and public sectors. She runs a private coaching and healing practice today. She feels that she is the sum of all that went before, wounds, "warts" and wonders, and is still growing, learning, healing, laughing, loving, and fully engaged with life, however it is unfolding. And she has every intention of leaving a legacy.

This conversation with Sylvia feels like we are sitting together on a beach, staring at the ocean waves hitting the shore. It's a sunny day and Sylvia is wearing a dramatic pair of sunglasses and large dangling earrings, her words as captivating as she is.

We've enabled a disrespect towards elders in our society that I do not support or encourage. Sometimes there are kids on the sidewalk and they don't move aside to let me go through. I do not move off the sidewalk onto the road; I say, "Excuse me, could you move aside?" and I've had a few of them say, "Well, you know we have a right to be here," to which I reply, "You have a right to be here, but I had a responsibility to pay for this, the sidewalk you're standing on, I helped pay for it therefore I fulfilled my responsibility, I paid for my rights; you have not yet paid. I'm fine with you not having paid, but you defer to me, I don't defer to you." I find they usually move.

I have until recently worked in corporate organizational development and in that workplace there are now three generations with the Baby Boomers retiring out. There are a lot of young people, perhaps 20 to 30 years younger than me. There were obvious generational differences and very often, they reacted to it. Sometimes I noticed it because at 47, you can't know what you know at 67. This is impossible. There are times when I have to remind myself that the stuff they don't seem to know, is really because they can't yet know it. I had an experience in my coaching practice when I was coaching two 18-year-old girls and one of them said to me, "I know there's more to life than this, but I can't quite figure it out." She just hasn't had enough experience of the world. But to know that at 18, that's amazing!

I don't like the word "aging." I am not aging; I'm getting older. "Aging" seems to have a meaning, for our western world, of diminishment, of losing your mental capabilities and physical capacity, becoming very needy, being reliant on others. I'm not losing capability or capacity, I'm gaining both: I study, I learn, I apply it to my coaching and healing practice, I'm in better shape now than I was 30 years ago. For me "old" is a mindset, it is people of any age who have a tendency to be very stuck in a way of being, set in their ways, a willingness to sit around and do little, very sure that they are right and not much openness to difference and possibilities, self-absorbed and convinced they are entitled to a certain level of comfort and personal enjoyment.

I don't go out specifically to "seniors" things. I got an invitation from Revera Homes, which is a conglomerate that runs seniors homes and care homes for elders. They had "just the place for me"! They got my name from the electoral roll and they invited me to a luncheon. "For Chrissakes," I replied. "Don't invite me to a luncheon. I don't want to go to your luncheon. I am fundamentally, totally uninterested." I just turned 70, but I don't go out to "seniors luncheons." I don't do "seniors fitness," I do Zumba dancing with 20-somethings because that's my capacity and capability. I run 6k every other day, and in the intervening days I stretch and lift weights.

I have more fear of aging than I do of dying, of the illnesses and emotional effects of aging that appear to be the norm in our culture. I found I was becoming fearful of doing things I used to do all the time: going to the movies alone, going out in the evenings by myself, going out to run on a day when it's snowy or the sidewalk is icy. I started to restrict my life and I realized that I needed a very different model or else I'd end up exactly where I didn't want to be. I'm after quality of life; longevity without quality of life does not interest me. Longevity, having more life, is what our scientists and the medical profession seem to be aiming towards with all the research they do, with their drugs and "interventions." I want them to clearly understand that I don't want more life unless I have a high quality of life.

I have a tendency to avoid old people! My best friends are ten years younger than me, and they are brilliant men and women who have achieved a great deal in their lives, for themselves. They're proud of what they're doing, and they are all engaged in a sense of contribution and participation in the world around them. I do have a friend who is in her 90s and who still goes out to participate publicly, regardless of weather, when issues of great concern evolve into public demonstration. She is my model; she is my hero.

I found my own role models of aging. I mean people like Jane Goodall. And Maria Gomori, who teaches the Virginia Satir method and is 92 years old. She travels to China several times a year for work. Isn't that exciting?! And she's very attractive, beautiful like a 92-year old who's taken care of herself, still finds joy and pleasure in life and is fully engaged in the world. When asked how she stayed so vital and alive after 92 years, she said the key to living a full life for all your years is being congruent with yourself, telling yourself your truth. So that's what I try to do. And it isn't always easy!

One of the things I did quite early on was I determined that I was going to have a purpose and an intention to contribute and participate in the world to take me through to the end of life. So I'm not withdrawing from life because I'm past 65, not going to play golf or spend half my year in Florida. I have a responsibility to model a more respectful and healthful approach to growing older for my children and grandchildren, and I take that responsibility quite seriously.

A lot of women who become mothers forget that that's just a role. I raised my kids not to engage with me as "Mommy." I'm not "Mommy" — I don't act like "Mommy." For a while when they were teens I had them call me by my first name. I kept saying to them, "You have to understand, my role relationship to you is 'Mommy,' but I'm actually a person with a life." Kids don't actually get an opportunity, even adult kids, to see their parents as real people with real lives and real excitement and passion about all aspects of life.

I dealt with my kids with increasing equality as they matured. When my teenage son, who is the eldest of the kids, was getting a little pushy, one of the things my daughters and I used to say was, "If you keep that up we will tell you about our sex lives!" And the look on his face! "No, that's okay," he'd mumble as he walked away. It was very funny! When I saw the look on his face I turned to my daughter and said, "Okay, let's remember that one!" So now all three and their partners find it's much more interesting to engage with me as a person with a life. There's nothing much in my life that they don't know. As a matter of fact, nowadays, they are as much my resources as I am for them.

Right now I am surrogate parent to my grandchildren. I'm not just a grandmother; I'm kind of the third "parent." My role as grandmother is getting clearer and clearer. I'm not expected to set the rules and guidelines by which my daughter-in-law and son want their kids to grow up, but I am expected and asked to reinforce their principles. I have to enable and support them doing a great job as parents. It's not my way; it has to be their way. My role as a grandmother is to love my grandchildren unconditionally and provide options to the guidance of their parents.

For example, I have a 3-year-old granddaughter and she loves to whine to get her own way. So she and I are practicing negotiation. She'll whine at me about something and I'll say, "That's not going to work."

And she'll say, "But I waaaant iiiit."

So I'll say, "Sorry, that isn't going to work with me. Would you like to negotiate?"

She'll look at me and say, "Yes!"

So I teach her how to negotiate. And it's not as though she gets her way when she negotiates. She gets more of her way, because it's a two-way street.

Being an elder in the fullest sense of that word is my job. It's my job to experience this latter part of life my way, and then communicate what I've done, why I've done it, how I've done it and what's the outcome for me, so that people can make better, informed choices. I didn't think of aging as a negative thing until I experienced it. When I was 63 or 64, I noticed that I had the same energetic will, but was forcing my capacity to demonstrate it. I remembered being a young, single mother of three children, making sure they got to all their activities, having a full-time job, having a social life of my own and not finding that necessarily exhausting. So I recognized that something significant had shifted. I also experienced losing a thought, not being able to remember a word or finding myself at the top of the stairs and wondering why I had come up here. I did not love that experience.

I don't like the medical model of aging and the way medicine approaches it. When I turned 65, every health professional that I went to see talked differently to me. It started off with, "At your age, you should be taking this medicine, you should be doing that, you shouldn't be doing this," and that's just wrong because that's all stuff based on a statistical bell curve. I used to say to my doctor, "I'm not on your bell curve. Do not treat me that way." I don't see the medical profession as being the expert in MY aging. I am also very clear that I am not your "patient." "Patient" implies a hierarchical, passive relationship, where I, who am paying, am lower than you who are offering the service. That is not right. I am a peer to you. You have medical training, I am the expert in this body and I make the decision, not you. I'm the one who gets to live with the consequences of those decisions, not anybody else.

The response of the medical profession to anything that involves aging is often to prescribe drugs, which deplete the body, and that's very hard to recover from, so my choice has been to go the alternative route. I pay for it because the government health insurance program won't cover anything "alternative." The medical profession doesn't particularly like this approach and my GP at the time wanted me to sign a piece of paper that says she's told me what she wants me to do and I've chosen not to do it, so that she's not at fault. I take full responsibility for my health; I'm informed. I use food, supplements and alternative healing methodologies to manage growing older. I began to explore bioidentical hormones with a doctor who is very knowledgeable in anti-aging medicine, and am on bioidentical hormones now. It's made a huge difference for me. I've actually documented my journey with bioidentical hormones and published it, and I talk about it with anybody who's interested.

The best thing about getting older is that I have the wisdom to know that I have no advice to give to anybody. There is a wisdom that comes with growing older. I'd love to have the energy of 30 with the wisdom of 70. When you're 30, you can't look forward and see what you will become. At 70, life is a whole lot less painful and you have the perspective of looking back at yourself with compassion and appreciation for all that you've overcome and created, and the "you" that you have become.

Part of the hard thing about getting older is being alone. Being alone is not something we're good at. We're conditioned to be in a relationship with a partner. I've spent the last five years getting as comfortable as I can get with being on my own. Now even when I'm lonely and alone, I'm fine. And most of the time, when I'm alone I love the company I keep!

When I was a kid it was an adult culture, and now we're a youth culture. I'm not sure it's good for anybody. I prefer the Indigenous cultures that value and respect every stage of life. I don't think any one stage should be ignored or disrespected.

I have had a few challenging transitions. One was when I left my ex and we divorced. I only took the kids — no money, no property — so that we didn't have to fight. Maybe that was a financially dumb decision, but my children were fine. Also, when my last child left home, left the city and moved out of the province, that was a very hard transition for me and took a long time to adjust to. Then when I lost my job with the company, I really suffered because I had an important role in this work community that disappeared. That was very hard — I actually had an emotional crash at that time. What I discovered was it's very easy to see yourself successful in a role, but it's much more meaningful and useful to be successful just for who you are as a person.

Lots of different things helped me get through these transitions: really good counselling, personal-growth programs, a few very good friends. I'm prone to depression, so I did take anti-depressant medication for a couple of years, which worked for me and then I got off them. When I discovered my own inner resources, that was pretty spectacular. What I learned from these transitions is that there are a lot of resources, that there's a lot of wisdom available if you search for it and that there isn't much I can't get through.

I'm not sure that I saw my parents aging — my father died when he was 57, my mother died at 69. By the time I was in my early 30s, I had lost about 14 members of my family and extended family, and that included both of my parents. So death was the theme of my childhood, not of my older years. Cancer and heart disease were the two big ones in my family, those deaths were ugly and horrible, took a long time and everybody suffered. So much of how you learn about death depends on how people around you behave. For me, death is terrifying. Everybody I know who died suffered a horrible death. As a family, we did not know how to grieve and how to help each other, especially how to help the children, so the people who suffered the most were us children. I've spent much time personally dealing with these issues, doing personal-growth work to deal with the stuck places along the grieving process and with my fear of death, because they affect how you engage with life.

I like our Northern First Nations and their ancient ways of dying. When I know I'm near death, I want to go out and lie down in the snow. That's the way I want to die. Or not necessarily in the snow — sand would be nice! Play me Mendelssohn's Violin Concerto, surround me with sunlight and warmth, warm air, take me to a mountaintop so I can smell the junipers. I'd like to die quietly, peacefully, without pain, without drugs and without machinery. If that could be arranged, that would be lovely.

I'm looking to go to a funeral home to talk about my death and dying process, and about how to set up my funeral. In the Jewish faith, you're buried within 24 hours, in a pine box, so I want a combination of the Jewish version and cremation, which is not part of Jewish tradition — which is weird! I want to be buried within 24 hours, no show, don't put me on display. If you couldn't see me when I was alive, you do not need to see me when I'm dead, because I'm not there. And then I want to be cremated. My kids know they are to spread my ashes, preferably in the Rockies or in the Gatineau hills. That is what I want. That is what I know they will do.

I don't know what comes after death ... however, if reincarnation works and the Deity asks me if I want to come back to earth in physical form, I will jump up and shout, "YES!" Life is an amazing experience and I wish to continue that journey.

THE INVITATION

12

Joanne's Story

Joanne is the 65-year-old mother of four daughters, mother-in-law to two, and grandmother to three. She is a former nurse and teaching assistant who loves children. She loves to listen to all of her daughters talking and laughing together, and being with her grandchildren. Joanne is an avid life-long volunteer who sees volunteering as a way to give back to her community. She enjoys driving around the countryside and stopping to take photographs when she sees something interesting. The most influential person in her life is her mother — the positive and the negative of her. She loves wearing pyjamas, sweatpants and her "mothers ring" with all her daughters' birthstones in it.

I imagine that we are having our conversation outdoors. It is a warm summer day, and we are sitting in a park filled with the sounds of birds chirping and her three grandchildren playing nearby.

I look at people who are in their 80s, going around with their walkers and canes, and it scares me because I'm getting closer to it. It's really hard to realize that I have more time behind me than I have ahead of me. I've lived for 65 years now; I don't have 65 years in front of me. I have more aches and pains now and I'm afraid of getting to the place of frailty. Even though my dad lived to be 91 years old, life is still short. I remember being 18, graduating from high school and feeling like I had

JOANNE'S STORY

my whole life ahead of me. I'm now 65 years old, and it scares me that it went by so quickly! My oldest daughter is 43, yet I feel like she was just born!

My parents never talked about aging. When my mom turned 70, she was in a rotten mood that day. I remember having her over for dinner and she was, oh my gosh, she was just in a rotten mood. She didn't want to turn 70. She wouldn't talk about it. She didn't talk about death and dying. I never saw my parents mourn their parents or their siblings when they died. I never heard my mother say that she missed either of her parents or her brother. So when my mother died, the five of us kids had no clue about how to mourn or how to grieve because we hadn't been taught.

There was a paramount event in my life that made me aware of my age. It was 12 years ago, six weeks before I turned 53. My husband of 32 years came home and said, "I've changed my mind. I don't love you anymore and I'm leaving." He literally took my world away. We have four daughters and he left me for someone who's just eight years older than my oldest daughter. I remember saying to him, "I have given you my whole adult life." And he said, "Oh yeah, you did." What was I supposed to do? Because I'd always been someone's daughter, someone's wife, or someone's mother. Who was I supposed to be at the age of 53? That was a time in my life when I became very conscious of my age.

Another time I was aware of my age happened right before that, when my oldest daughter told us that she was pregnant. At that time, I remember realizing my own mortality because there I was at 52 — how long was I going to have with this grandchild? I thought I better become a very healthy person so that I stay around.

My whole adult life had been my family — my husband and the kids came first — that was it. I never wanted to be alone. My youngest had just moved out of the house and here I wound up alone, and this was never what I wanted!

It was the most challenging transition in my life because I had to completely rebuild myself. I found a counsellor who was phenomenal. I decided that I was going to try different things to help me along: past-life regression, soul retrieval, Landmark Forum, reading a lot of self-help books. I relied on my girls and on their companionship, so I had them help me through it too. I was fortunate that I have friends who put their lives on hold to help me, to keep me glued together. I had a lot of support from people at my work. I took three weeks off — I couldn't go to work. The love and support I got from all these different parts of my life, from people and from God, helped me get through this. I was born and raised a Catholic, but I had gotten away from the church. I found, especially at the beginning, that I needed to go and just sit in church. I would go to the same place all the time, and I would sit there and cry, but when I left, I felt good.

It's still a process, even though it's been over ten years. Some of the damage that was done cannot be healed. When my husband did this, he literally took my world away because I had no clue. I think part of the recovery was to do things I felt I couldn't do. I had relied on him to drive during vacations, so that first summer I decided to visit two of my daughters, who both lived far away. I was gone for two weeks. I drove to one daughter's home in Knoxville, Tennessee, then drove to my second daughter's home in Amelia Island, Florida, and then back. I drove 3500 miles all by myself! When I got home, I said to myself, "Oh my god! I did this!" I think part of the recovery was discovering that I had a strength in me I never knew I had. A lot of getting through the hard times is finding the strength that you really have inside, and, to me, God plays a big part of it. I've always been a family person, but I appreciate it more now. I think I appreciate now just about everything that I took for granted before. I had always planned on growing old with him. We had plans for retirement. Then all of a sudden I had to look at things completely differently. That transition opened my heart. Yes, I've gained a lot.

I believe things happen for a reason. I will have to die and hopefully

I'll go to Heaven, and then I'll find out why this happened. I have no answers to it right now. None. I still don't understand it.

My mom died when she was 80 of a brain tumour. In February 1998, my mom was having terrible headaches that were diagnosed as sinus infections. By the end of March she had neurological signs in her face, left leg and arm that I thought had been caused by a stroke. I was the one who took her for the CT scan that found a brain tumour. The nurse took me aside to talk with the doctor. He told me I would have to tell my mom about the tumour, and that she would have to be admitted into the hospital for a few days so medication could be monitored.

I felt crushed in so many ways and didn't know what to do. In the space of a few seconds, I decided not to tell her about the tumour until my dad arrived and could be with her at the hospital. I said to her, "The doctor wants to do more testing, so we need to admit you." She got angry with me. She said she was not going to be admitted and would walk home. The nurse talked her into staying.

When I walked with her over to admissions, the new nurse asked for her name and said to her, "You mean they didn't bring you over in a wheelchair? You walked over here with a mass that size?!" And my mother looked at me, so I had to sit her down and tell her. Oh my god. Oh my god. And my dad wasn't there. It was awful for her to hear that news. She stayed in the hospital for four days. On April 18, 1998, Mom had surgery to remove the tumour. Not all of it could be taken out, so about five weeks later she started radiation. The radiation made her feel sick and proved to be of no help to her. Two weeks after she stopped radiation she started showing symptoms again. Another CT scan showed the tumour was back, and bigger than before.

The doctor said she'd probably have about two weeks, and that's exactly what she had to the day. He said to us, not to her, to us, "This will be her time to get her ducks in order, to say to people what she wants to say." She would have none of it. None of it because she wouldn't acknowledge that there was anything wrong. Because if you acknowledge it, then it's true and you're going to go. I don't think she said goodbye to anybody. She never had conversations with any of us that were, "When I'm gone..." or, "I'd like you to have blah blah..." None of that happened.

In the last two weeks of her life my mother was in a hospital bed in her home and we went through hospice. I believe that just because someone is sick doesn't mean you have to put them in a nursing home or hospital. You keep them in the home and take care of them. By training, I'm a nurse, so I moved in. I was the basic caretaker for my mother for her last two weeks. I had one brother who just couldn't handle it, so he didn't come. I don't think it was until afterwards, when I became involved as a volunteer with hospice, that I realized he couldn't handle it. It wasn't that he was staying away because he didn't care — he couldn't handle it. But like I said, we didn't know how to talk about it, how to mourn her.

She was bedridden at home for those two weeks and she fought so hard. She didn't want to leave. She died on a Thursday, and on the Monday beforehand her breathing became so laboured. She fought for every breath she took. You could tell she was in so much pain. She wasn't conscious, but anytime we had to move her she would wince and make a noise. She just wouldn't give up and go.

At the beginning, we thought she was waiting for one of her grandsons and his family. He came that Saturday, and we thought that after the visit she would go and she didn't! Everyone had come to see her who was going to see her, so I really can't figure it out. I know my younger sister told her it was okay to go and she still stayed. I don't know what was keeping her here. I often wonder about that. But she wasn't one to say goodbye to anybody — she didn't with any of us. The day my mother, their grandmother, died, the hospice nurse said to one of my daughters, "Your mother just handed you a legacy by showing you how this should be done."

At the time, I was of the thinking that you had to be with a loved one when they died. So I made sure there was someone with her, every second, because I couldn't stand the thought of her dying with nobody there. In the last week she was alive, there were 14 of us that were there in that house all the time. During my self-exploration, I came to realize that you don't die alone. You may not have people within the physical world, this world, with you but there are people on the other side waiting for you, they're with you when you go, so you're not alone.

In my last meaningful conversation with her she was still upset that I didn't bring her home when she was diagnosed with the brain tumour. Even after everything she went through, she was still stuck on the fact that I didn't take her home. In my dark moments I think, "Oh my god, she felt that way about me. What is she going to say to me if I see her, when I see her again?" Hopefully she won't be upset anymore. I don't know if it can be taken away now. I don't know how to alter that memory. I don't know how to explain it to myself. I think she was very scared. And there's so much we don't know because she just never spoke of that.

I started volunteering at the hospice, Hospicare, after my mother died. When she was dying we had a wonderful nurse helping us and everyone at the agency was wonderful. I wanted to give back to the agency; we couldn't have kept her at home without their help. Hospice has really influenced me. I witnessed older people die gracefully. You can die at any age. You can do it gracefully. There's a grace to it. I guess I didn't see that with my mother because she was fighting so hard. She wouldn't let go. And I think there comes a time when you have to let go in the dying process.

Then my dad lived alone until he was 91, almost 92, but I didn't consider him old because he was a single man, living by himself. I helped with grocery shopping and taking care of him. He fell, broke his hip and died four weeks later.

Two nights before my dad died, he was having a really bad night and the nurse called me and asked me if I'd come in. I did and was with him all night long. He was restless and he kept talking about the light over in the corner. I kept fighting within myself — should I tell him it's okay to go? Oh I can't. Oh, should I?

At about three a.m., I finally leaned down and said, "Dad, it's okay to go."

His eyes flew open. He looked at me and asked, "What did you say?"

I said, "Oh, it's okay to go to sleep."

And he said, "Oh, okay." He quieted right down and slept the rest of the night.

I think that's when he started to decide that it was okay for him to go. I gave him permission. No one else was there who would do that. I had so much turmoil within me before I did it. After, I felt a sense of relief. I felt that I had done what I was supposed to do.

I think he chose to die because the doctors said to me, "Oh, he's not going anywhere for a long time," and the next day he was gone. I want to be able to let go like my dad did. I had the best evening with him before he died, the best time — we laughed!! Luckily, I told him things that I hadn't told him yet and we just laughed!! I gave him a piece of candy and told him not to put the whole thing into his mouth because he would choke, and he did, and we laughed about it. Little did I know that that would be the last time I would see him alive.

After my dad died, the family fell apart. My mother had been the glue that had kept the five of us siblings together and then my father took over that role. I learned a lot when my dad died about the possessions in the house and the problems they can cause in the family. I lost a sister over material things when my dad died. I mean it's utterly ridiculous that it's over material things. And I wasn't even the executor! My sister has nothing to do with any of her siblings, any of her family anymore. Recently I was very upset by this when my other sister, Suzy, was here, and we went to visit our relatives. One cousin said to the two of us, "Well, how's your sister?" Suzy said, "Oh, we don't have a sister," and my mouth opened. My cousin looked at me with huge eyes and I didn't say anything. I took a step back; I didn't want to be associated with that because yes, I do have a sister, but she has chosen to do it this way to get through it. I often think of her, I mourn her, I send her pictures and things that I find around the house, and I never hear from her. This is a loss of her choosing, not giving any of us a chance to sit down and have a conversation. She lives away and I remember saying to her one time, "Let's meet halfway and not come out of that hotel room until this is taken care of." She won't acknowledge anything anymore. She thinks what she thinks, and that's all she wants to know. It's more painful because it's preventable. She's not ready, and I don't know if she ever will be. She's two years older than I am, so she's 67, and I often think when she gets ill are we even going to know? And then what will I do? And when she passes away, what will I do? Will we even know? And that is so horrible! Because it's preventable.

I remember being younger and not wanting to deal with death and dying. When I bring it up, my daughters just don't want to talk about it because then it makes it real, that you really could go. And I keep saying, if you plan it, then it's easier in the end. You don't have to worry about A, B, C, or D, it's taken care of, then you can mourn and not deal with these other things. I don't want what happened with my sister to happen with my daughters. I don't want anybody to go through that. There's no question about what's going to happen. Because when a person dies within a family, things can happen and you lose your remaining family over it.

So I told my daughters, "I'm not your glue. You guys have to do this yourselves." What I have done is get everything set. I have all my papers together, I went through my home and took pictures of everything that's important to me, gave a copy to each daughter and said, "You tell me now what you want." They each did and there was one item that more than one of them wanted — I did a lottery. So I have the list along with the pictures with all my papers. I don't have to worry about that. All my papers are in order — my insurance, my bank account, everything. All my funeral arrangements are made — everything.

One day I said to my eldest that I want to be cremated and I want my ashes scattered. They know this; I have instructions written down and money set aside.

I said, "So I've decided that I would like each of you, if you have an opportunity, to plant a tree somewhere instead of my having a stone anywhere."

My oldest daughter said to me, "If you don't have a stone, where will we go to visit?"

I said, "You won't. The tree will be your reminder when you want to visit me. Just look at the tree and remember me. That's what I want you to do."

For me, death itself isn't scary — it's the getting there. I want to be able to know I'm going, and I want to be able to say goodbye to those that I want to and then go. I just want to go peacefully. I can be alone when that happens. I fear it and I don't want to feel desperate, I want to feel ready for it to come. I think that's what my dad did.

# 13

Jane's Story

Jane is a 68-year-old enthusiastic and ever-curious participant in life, with all its ups and downs. Her career has been focused in the world of business, including working for a high tech firm doing lead generation. Jane has been ahead of the curve, and with her skills and talent has had no difficulty being and staying employed. She also pursued a dream to be a singer. She took lessons, got a jazz repertoire and had some success doing this part-time. Jane joined AA at age 30 and has been sober over 37 years. She quit smoking a couple of years later and has continued for 35 years. She joined OA in 2013, since she is a sugar/junk food addict, and has lost 20 pounds. The most influential people in her life are her father, her grade five teacher, Miss Craik, and her first boss.

I feel like we are in Jane's kitchen; I'm sitting at her kitchen table and we're drinking freshly brewed coffee. She has her ironing board set up, her iron is ready and a pile of shirts is waiting, as she begins to share her story.

My mother was never an overly vain woman and felt there was nothing to be worried about in getting older. In fact she used to joke about it, calling herself, "your poor old Mother." She was very easygoing about it. If her hair went white, it went white. She was an energetic woman, always busy.

JANE'S STORY

My dad died at 50, many years ago. Unfortunately, my mother fell eight years ago, broke her shoulder and has never been the same. It's probably because she didn't do physiotherapy. The injury was probably very painful, especially given the fact that this happened when she was 80. So now she's appearing old. I'm impatient with her because I know she could have improved with physio. I really have to accept that she's frail. I see the folks at my mom's long-term care facility and I think it would be horrible to be confined to a wheelchair, but these folks don't seem un-cheerful. They have nice staff who look after them. I think of being debilitated, not being able to walk, but who knows? Maybe I'd love it. I do so love to sit!

When I see older people and what becomes of a lot of them — they look bent-over and their walking is more laboured — it's sad. I feel bad for them. I try to remember, "You know, you're going to be there someday." I think maybe that won't happen to me because I'm healthy, but none of us knows. It's strange to see the way a face ages and wrinkles. There's an "Oh, I don't want to be like that" feeling. I find some older people seem down or don't look people in the eye, so maybe there is a depression that comes with it. If they're upright and walking along, I'm happy for them. I feel a bit guilty if I see them looking pained or hunched over. I can only hope that with the attitudes I've developed, old age won't impact me as much, that I'll have good friends and good ways to deal with it.

Health is everything, mental health, too, and not worrying too much. I have to stay healthy otherwise I'm not going to feel good. And I hate feeling bad. I start feeling very depressed and it can happen quickly, so I'm careful with myself. I appreciate peace of mind. Through my time in AA (Alcoholics Anonymous) and after I quit smoking, I discovered it's so nice not to have that squirrely mind, to be calm, take the next step, do the next right thing. But I've stood on the shoulders of giants; I didn't do any of this by myself. An awful lot of this was through the wisdom in the rooms of AA. It's not just that you stop drinking, it's that you really grow if you work at it. And I guess I really needed to because I was a very hyper and unhappy person. I've been in AA for almost 38 years. I came in young, before anything too awful could happen. I behaved like an idiot and I am an alcoholic, which is an interesting thing. What's become evident to me is that these 12 steps are helpful for anyone because we're all powerless over something.

The other fellowship I'm in has to do with food and sugar. I really hit bottom. I can binge on sugar, gaining and losing weight. When I was a child, I was what they would call "a big girl." I lost a lot of weight from diet pills when I was 13, so my appearance has always been important to me. It's a little bit more fear-based than I wish it was, but that's the way I am. I could eat endless cookies and taco chips, so I just said I have to cut this out and went to OA (Overeaters Anonymous). That's really been my whole social network — AA and OA — which is a bit limiting. I am no longer involved in OA at this point, and have not binged at all. I think I did learn a lot in that fellowship, but I only go to AA now.

I haven't dated in years, nor do I want to; I am happy with friendships. And I'm not really talking much to my family. I don't know what it is. I think my sister and I have addiction issues, and she is very much in her own world; she has three kids. I used to think we were close and we're not "not" close, but I don't think we are terribly interested in each other's lives at the moment. That sounds harsh I know. We're both pretty strong personalities, so that's probably part of it. We do love each other, we just don't see that much of each other currently.

I noticed, even as early as 45 years old, that I was strongly considering plastic surgery because I thought, "Gasp! I'm getting that double chin! Oh NO!" For me, it had to do with being pretty, since I felt so plain and almost ugly as a young girl. During that stint of wanting plastic surgery, I realized that it cost way too much money and I gave up on the idea. The harder things about getting older are seeing the changes in your body, not only the "softening jaw line," but the upper arms, the flab, that kind of thing. I never was a *"Baywatch"* girl — still, it takes longer to work off stuff. I try not to let it get to me.

I think you have to connect with other people. I was a very self-centered young woman; self-involved, apathetic, had no goals. All I cared about was how I looked and how much money I was going to make, but I was very upset inside and of course I loved to drink. I know now that isolation of spirit is a killer.

As an older woman, sometimes I was conscious of my age at work. My co-workers were in their 30s and 40s, and sometimes I felt a bit nutty, but I liked being the nutty, older one. I'd say, "It's because I'm a crazy old broad!" I think that's ridiculous because I don't believe that, I just did it to get a laugh out of people.

The best thing about getting older is continuing to grow emotionally and spiritually. It's the personal growth work I've done to really know who I am. There is also the wisdom that comes with aging. Even if you don't do the inner work on yourself, you do get to know what you want to do and what you don't want to do, your likes and dislikes. You learn how to step away from situations without anger and know what's not for you, letting it go at that. The unexamined life is not worth living. Don't try to fill that hole with a pair of shoes. Take a look at what's really going on, and get therapy if you need it.

As I got older, I thought, I wonder if I will retire? I had never really thought about retirement before. I guess everyone thinks it would be wonderful to have lots of money, be on a beach or something like "Freedom 55." Going to work kept me going. I know it's important for me to be with people and not sit at home and watch TV. That would be pretty bad.

I went from working full-time to working part-time, two days a week. I was working from home, but found it increasingly challenging to not speak with anybody in person. It was harder to motivate myself when I was not around people, so I decided to retire fully. And it was nice! I didn't have to wake up at 6:30 in the morning anymore! Sleeping in was one of the big benefits, and having all the time in the world, not having to go anywhere or do anything.

I really didn't miss work. I just needed to find some other outlets, so I applied to volunteer at various hospitals and was accepted as an orientation host. I volunteered in the winter but after a few months I decided to go back to my old company for two days a week to help me not go through my retirement funds as quickly. It has been great to see all my workmates and there are new things to learn, so it is good for my brain!

It's sad because I'm very lonely at times. There's not a lot I want to do, I have to force myself to do stuff. Ever since I was a teenager this apathy has been an issue, and feeling uninvolved is coming up again, but once I get up and going it's okay. I work out every other day, and I have my 12-step program, so I go to meetings. I started to go to church every Sunday and to a Bible study mid-week — this has really meant a lot to me — I feel connected to God and I no longer have that depression and fear. I think you have to reach out and love. If you don't love, your life will fly by you. You have to love something other than yourself. Love is the answer. It really is — love is the answer.

I know though that all humans go through these dark nights of the soul. I turn to the Bible for help. I think it is the Dalai Lama who says he forces himself to think he's going to die, to be aware of it each day as a little reminder. So I've done that and it helps to keep it simple. Death was the biggest mystery in the world to me, but not now, since I started studying the Bible. I believe John 3:16 — it's a goodie!

I haven't done anything to prepare myself. I don't want to think I'm not going to be able to make my own decisions, that I'm going to get dementia. It may be too early for me. As I feel decrepitude happening, maybe I'll think about it more then. I'm going to make a decision to make no decision because it doesn't feel close enough. I should do a will but I find it costs a lot. You can get them done for $400 or you can do them for nothing, and that may be the way I go. I still have to decide how to divide up any of an estate I might have left. Some to charities, for sure. I should sit down and do that. It's just that it's work.

I did give some thought to whom I would ask about my powers of attorney (for personal care and for finances). I thought of a few people, but none of them seem quite right. My financial planner, who is a very good business guy and is quite warm, would probably be good as the financial POA. My sister could probably do the care thing if she is willing. She has both health and finance POA for my mother. My brother and I are co-executors of my mother's will. My sister looks after my mother's long-term care and how they're doing it: when her nails are cut, paying the bills, that kind of thing. Luckily we do have a lot of trust in the family. I know my sister would never touch a dime herself, which doesn't always happen as we know. I thought of asking a dear friend, but she's around my age. My sister has tacitly said, sure if that's what you want. I think she knows what decisions I would want made on my behalf.

I do believe there's something after death; I want to believe that. Maybe I'm in denial, maybe because it hasn't been close to me, but they say it's just another transition. I have a faith in God and Christ, and that helps me. But I have no idea and I don't want to think about it much. I'm not looking forward to a lot of discomfort. When you're lying on that bed and taking the last few breaths, it might be scary. I would like to die very peacefully, in bed after an illness, I guess, or just seeing the final breaths go. Just peacefully.

At any rate, as I say, my feelings of worry have mainly been dissolved by my faith in Jesus, and I thank God for that. It's very important to have a faith in something greater than yourself, call it what you will — the life force, the collective humanity. It really is amazing to think about it, that this is going to end. I really hope there's something else other than this, and I hope that I go there and I hope it's good.

Just prior to printing the book, I sadly learned that Jane died. Her generosity, bright smile and quick sense of humour stay with me, and I'm ever grateful that she contacted me on 11/11/11 to participate in this project. I hope Jane did go where she wished to when she died, and that it is very good.

THE INVITATION

14

RUTH'S THOUGHTS ON DEATH: WHAT I MISSED

Where are you, Dad?
Dead, my darling.

People sent me such thoughtful, loving notes after my dad died. I was in pain and spoke about it with anyone who was ready to listen. They shared all kinds of comforting ideas: that he was with me, that he will always be with me, that he will visit me, that he has visited me, that he is still here only in a different way, that my memories of him will comfort me, that the Jewish mourning rituals will be healing and a helpful way to mark my grief.

Nope.

None of that happened for me.

He wasn't beside me.

He wasn't in me.

He wasn't with me. He wasn't with me when the first Father's Day arrived.

He wasn't sending me messages.

That was what was so sad for me. That was what I was grieving.

In the weeks before he died, my dad said, "Dying is not a pleasure. There is no continuation. I am saddened to leave you."

He did not believe there is anything after death, not with his many losses in life and his own near-deaths. And honestly, I did not experience his continuation — not as a spirit, not as a guide, not as a ghost.

He died and was gone from the living.

He didn't visit me.

He didn't speak to me.

He died and I had to let go.

I felt the loss of him. I missed his essence and his presence. What are they after someone dies?

I don't believe my dad died to go somewhere better. Somewhere better was right beside his wife; it was with his family.

There is a competitive game of grieving.

How are you grieving? What are you doing to grieve?

How much are you grieving? How horrific is your grief?

Are you doing the right things to grieve?

Are you writing up an impressive obituary, following the proper rituals of mourning?

Are you grieving normally? Is your grief complicated?

How fast can you heal? How soon can you get back to work?

How long can you grieve? How far can you stretch it out?

How strong, stoic, courageous are you in your grief?

How evolved can you be in your grief?

How productive can you be during grief?

How much pain can you endure?

How [shocking, awful, beautiful, extraordinary] is your grief?

We are expected to be strong, to forge through, to wear a mask of "I'm fine," while our blood sugars surge with the stress, while our saliva acidifies from the sorrow and our cells weep themselves to sleep.

I was just trying to figure out what was my way, how did I grieve, what helped and didn't help me. It was a process, to let go of my dad, to allow the sadness and missing to exist, be felt and known, and then fade into life. The thing I know now is that there are insights and experiences during the process that are magical, profound and incredibly painful.

Sometimes grief was a bad dance partner, overpowering and distracting me from my life. I wanted to know how long grieving would take, how long it would last, that it was going to end, and that it would end sooner rather than later.

My dad's death was crushed together with other family deaths, losses and transitions in the first couple of years. Grief was everywhere, around me and within me. I was offered books and resources, but had no interest. I couldn't find the attention or concentration to read them anyway. I was in it. This was it. What were these books and resources going to say to validate or confirm it? I did what I could to not turn away, not deny, not busy myself, not distract myself from the sorrow. I understood why people avoid and numb this pain of grief — it is unbelievable. There were moments when I easily could have lit up a spliff, or consumed boozy cocktails or platters of decadent desserts, or binge-watched television programs, or busied myself with work projects. I decided not to, and submerged myself. I tried to stay present to the grief. Sometimes it was very hard to be with the pain, so I made peace with being "here," moving through grief for however long it took and wherever it took me. Wherever I was, was fine.

While I was growing up, I saw my parents grieve in many different ways: through storytelling, by sharing their memories of the relationship with the person who had died and their regrets. There were no rituals or ceremonies or celebrations or traditions, but they showed me how they grieved in ways that were meaningful and personal for them. So I grieved my dad through stories, memories, and photos. I grieved through food and meals: schnitzel and cucumber salad, chicken paprikash and dumplings, Chinese food and falafel sandwiches, honey cake and mint tea, espresso and mocha torte. I grieved by listening to familiar folk songs and classical music: Nana Mouskouri, Pete Seeger, Dvorak and Beethoven. The way I grieved my dad was as unique as my relationship with him. I think that's true for each of us; our grief is unique as we are and unique as the relationship.

I didn't anticipate the fog of grief. It felt like a constant heaviness inside me. I was exhausted on every level: emotionally, physically, spiritually, psychically, and psychologically. My energy was drained and I was spent. It was an abstract distractedness that came over me while I made sense of the loss.

I found myself showering twice, because I was not sure if I washed myself. As I turned off the shower taps, I wondered if I soaped myself so turned the water back on just in case.

I left my debit card in a store and only realized it at the end of the day.

I forgot to bring food to a potluck dinner.

I received a call from my local video store about two missing movies. I promised I had returned them. I did, but I had returned them to my local public library, not the video store.

The cognitive fog stayed for months and months until one day I noticed it wasn't there. I knew that I had soaped myself in the shower. I didn't forget my debit card anywhere again. My concentration and focus returned. The energetic sensitivity faded and I was able to be in groups of people and noisier environments without become agitated or distracted. The emotional heaviness faded as birthdays, holidays and anniversaries of his illness arrived and passed. I was integrating my dad's death into my life.

I used to think that hauntings were about ghosts in cemeteries and haunted houses but I experienced a different kind of haunting. They were uncomfortable, sometimes painful, memories of my dad's dying and death that lingered with me. There were haunting experiences that lingered: when he looked and sounded like he was in tremendous pain, conversations with hospital staff, the sight of him in the hospital room after he died. They stuck deep in my senses — the sights, smells, sounds, and emotions — and hung around for a long time, reminding me of those painful moments, wondering if he suffered, urging me to find inner peace.

Months after my dad died, he appeared in my dream. He was much younger, in his 50s, and his hair was brown again. He stood six feet tall, and wore a familiar outfit on his lean frame, a short-sleeved beige shirt with beige slacks. He was in a hospital cafeteria, like the one he used to take me to for a mid-morning snack when I was a child spending the day with him in the laboratory. I watched him from a distance; he was in conversation with his colleagues and friends. When he saw me, he came up to me and lovingly told me, "It's okay. Everything is okay." Even as I was dreaming, I wondered, was my dad really visiting me? Was he trying to console me and let me know he is okay? I believe it was my spirit consoling me, easing my distress and healing myself.

My dad asked me, repeatedly, to support my mom. He beseeched me, "Please be there for her when I'm gone."

"How, Dad?"

He nodded his head, "You know how."

I worried about what would happen to my mom after my dad died. She had lost her life partner and best friend of 64 years, and the routines and roles that were intertwined with his. How would she cope with the shock? I was scared that she would die soon after him — the way of many long-term marriages — and that I would lose her too.

She decided that she needed to move shortly after my dad died; the large suburban house haunted her with its memories of him. I did my best to be there for her. After she settled into her new downtown apartment, we spent valuable time together. We did grocery shopping together, went for manicures and pedicures, travelled to visit relatives, went to concerts, watched elections and the Olympics on her gigantic television, talked about her memoirs, dined out, invited each other over for meals, and had endless phone calls. She had a deep, dark vacuum where her relationship used to be and in that space our mother-daughter relationship had an opportunity to grow into something new. We connected in a way that was unburdened somehow, maybe the place my dad had in her life was now available to the world.

She taught me about resilience, compassion and courage. I appreciate every moment that I still have with her, two years after his death, and for our evolving relationship. A most beautiful part of losing my dad is how it brought my mom and me closer, how we moved from mother and daughter to being friends. I know soon enough I will be grieving her, too.

Then it hit me . . . the final insight I needed to make this book complete. I'd spoken about my grief with my family and close friends, but it is such a taboo to ask others about their grief that I didn't even think to include questions about it in the interviews. I could ask questions about aging and illness, death and dying, but not grief. Even while I was grieving, with grief all around me, I didn't ask the interviewees about grief. That is how terribly taboo grief is.

Grief is a deeply painful place, perhaps the most painful of places. To ask people about it felt inappropriate and unacceptable to me, like I was being rude or crossing an invisible line into people's way of coping with emotional pain. I felt like I was not supposed to ask them about their pain of loss, their pain of losing someone. But I did think of many interview questions I would have liked to ask, "What did you learn from your parents about grieving? How did they grieve?" and, "When in your life have you grieved?" and, "How did you experience the pain of grief?" These questions would have to be added to the list and included in the book.

ès

I miss my dad, but the quality of missing has shifted. The hauntings faded and when I think of my dad, which is not often really, it is with peace. My heart needed to feel fully and not be denied. Grief helped to shine light in the painful places of loss, illuminating what I missed, from the tiniest to the enormous. As I lived the loss of him, I learned what I appreciated: his enveloping hugs; his passion for politics and current events; his strong work ethic; his love for swimming in lakes; his knowledge of biochemistry, nutrition, and healing; his colourful curses; his love of coffee; his stubborn determination, deep responsibility, and gratitude for the wholeness in every moment. I see these as the many legacies he left me, and I continue to discover more of them as time passes. That is the wonder about losing someone you loved, continuing to realize the gifts they left you.

I now drive my dad's car. It is a small, silver sedan with the kind of low mileage that comes with riding around the neighbourhood. He loved to drive, leasing a new car every three years, after countless hours of research. He had all types of car gadgets, so when I turn on the seat warmer or put my hands on his steering wheel cover decorated with Canadian maple leafs, I feel I'm moving forward with his love and support. One day, I will ceremoniously drive his car in to purchase my swanky new vehicle. He'd love that.

❦

15

Doug's Story

Doug is a 48-year-old married man who is fascinated by what the world has to offer. He was born in Toronto and has lived there his whole life. He works as a law clerk in a government organization. A major belief of Doug's is that life is supposed to be fun, easy and meaningful, and partially made up as we go along. The most important people in Doug's life are his wife, his sister, his best friend Mike, his co-worker Cyd, his nephew Dan, and his mother, even though she isn't physically here. He loves going to Home Depot, travelling and being with friends as a couple.

Talking with Doug, I feel like we are on a fishing trip out in cottage country. Doug's family is up the hill in the cabin. We're casting. Doug gets the bait ready and we're drinking coffee early in the morning.

Losing my mom was a hard transition and extremely fulfilling, as well. I know that sounds weird, but my mom was in hospital for six months — I had a lot of time alone with her and had every question answered that I wanted answered. During the really hard moments, I would remind myself that things always change, so if today was a particularly hard day visiting my mom, I knew tomorrow wouldn't be the same day. It would be different. I could focus on losing my mom, but it was more beneficial for me to focus on the time that we had. I thought, these are my last chances and my last days to be with my mom. I wanted to ask all those questions nobody dared ask her, "What's this like for you?" and, "Are you afraid to die?" My dad and my siblings didn't do that. I was a bit nervous, but I prefaced it a few weeks earlier. I said, "I have lots of questions I want to ask you. Is it okay? I don't want to upset you." My mom was pretty good about it. I think in some ways she made it easy for me. The answers were what I thought they would be, but I wanted to ask someone who was going to die soon what that was like. She said she wasn't scared to die, but that she didn't want to because she didn't want to miss everything that was to come.

I went into the situation (of her dying) saying to myself that I didn't want to have any regrets. I think that's a good thing for life too — I don't want to have a regretful life. There's a sacredness to death and dying. I was the lucky one because everyone had fallen asleep and I couldn't fall asleep the night my mom died. It was a surreal moment because the person that died that night was just a body — my mom had left at least a day before her body died, and I knew that she had "left the building," so to speak, before she had actually died. My mom took care of her spiritual self, and her body took care of itself as it began to die — it was peaceful and meaningful. It was awful and very beautiful as well. The way it happened was incredibly enriching for me. It was quite an honour to witness it. She didn't fight it. I guess she accepted that she was going to die. It was probably one of the most valuable gifts I've ever received. It's a gift of a good relationship at a tough time. The most challenging moments of my life are almost always the moments I look back on with extreme gratitude. Funny I never really thought of it that way, but it's true. Gratitude is a big thing. You have to focus on looking for that golden nugget in a pile of crap.

Death is completely natural and a part of my life, so I want to honour that. I hope I can do the kind of job my mom did. I also realize it will be different. In some ways I think I'm dying a little bit every day, so I want to live well and enjoy my time. As my mom said, I'm not really afraid to die, I just don't want to yet. I don't know if there's ever a good time to die. I fear the "nuts and bolts" of it, how it is going to happen. I would like to die peacefully, without pain, honourably. I don't know that I want to die with a whole bunch of people around me, maybe just one person. In some ways I want to linger so I get to say all my good-byes. To die all of a sudden, and without warning, is hard on the people left behind. I would want them to know that they'll be okay and to help prepare them not to have any regrets once I'm gone.

I know this sounds weird, but many good things happen when a person dies, like the memories. I was blown away at my mom's funeral. So many people showed up and had stories to tell, stories that I hadn't heard of. We're so focused on how we want to change the world, there are all these hot shots out there trying to change the world and it's this big production. My mom wasn't like that at all, and man, did she change the world, unbeknownst to me and unbeknownst to even herself. It's surreal, how she changed people's lives and she didn't even know it. In my opinion, that's the best way to live life. I don't want to change someone's life like a Hollywood production. I just want to be myself and have that be a by-product. I know I've already done it. I don't know with whom or how, but I know I've done it a hundred times over just by being who I am. I know I've changed the world. The only problem is, you don't get to be at your own funeral! I got as close to my own funeral with my mom's. It's an amazing process.

As you get older more people die in your life. How do you cope with that? Everything changes when a family member dies. Everything is re-jigged. The dynamics and the system change, and it's quite surprising what happens. You can never predict the space that person held, positively or negatively. Things change in your life when someone leaves and it can catch you off guard. There have been huge shifts in my family as a result of my mom passing away. Things came up that I never saw and are all of a sudden right in my face.

Often you hear, "She was the glue of the family," but to experience it is eye-opening. It seemed like my dad really changed. Now I'm realizing that he didn't really change, what changed was how my mother kept my father in check. He had pretty narcissistic tendencies, which have really flourished because my mother is not here to tamp them down and do damage control.

It would be horrible to lose my wife and it would be horrible for her to lose me. I don't fear that though. There are beautiful parts to it too. I know there would be depth and soulfulness. Still I think it would be really hard to go through that grieving process.

Life is what you make of it. Dying, too, is what you make of it. It's your choice. When I was younger I didn't realize that was an option. I always thought that it was what life would give to me. As I get older, I realize there are a zillion options that I can give to my life, and I have the wisdom to know that things don't all have to change right now. I remember when I was younger my dad couldn't do things fast enough for me, he took his time, and I thought, "Oh my god, all these retired people! They've got all day to do this and they're so slow!" All I thought about was get the job done — get it done, get it done! That is the gift of getting older — do what you can do, there's always tomorrow to finish it — not the hardline, full-throttle pace. Now I think, "Yippee! I can take it nice and slow."

Aging opens up a whole new perspective. Life is more relaxed and peaceful. I don't worry so much. There is more depth and meaning to life. I'm learning to slow down physically, which also works mentally for me. It's weird that more time and space opens up, yet physically the time is decreasing because I'm getting closer to dying.

Now my body lets me know if I'm overdoing it! I ran a marathon a few years ago and I wasn't feeling well, I felt a little old. When I can't push through I get frustrated because 20 years ago I could. As the years go on, I'm having to listen to my body more. If you ask me, when am I old? Maybe it will be when I look in the mirror and I'm all wrinkled up. By that time, if you ask me the question again I'll probably say, "Oh, when I'm 90!"

The biggest fear I have about aging is I may not have younger friends to help me. When you're older and unable to do things, generally your children can help. We don't have any children, so that pops up every now and then. There's also the fear of losing mobility. Once mobility is gone, independence is gone. There's a fear that if my wife dies, I'll be alone. These fears are based around what I will lose. I tend to think of the fears and forget that there's a freer mentality when you're older.

I get more respect as an older man than I did as a younger man. Once I noticed it in my early 40s and I started carrying myself differently. I think my relaxed-ness came through, which put people at ease around me. Once people see that you're not trying to prove yourself anymore, it's like you've been proven.

My dad kind of minded aging. I think he wanted to be one of the younger guys; maybe there was some vanity there. I remember one time I introduced my dad to a friend and I said, "This is my dad. He's retired." And my dad flipped! He said, "I'm not retired! I work!" And I asked, "What do you do?" in front of my friend and my dad said, "I'm busy!" So I thought, "Oh. Okay, apparently he's not retired." Unknowingly I hit a real sore spot. I think he felt less-than because he no longer worked and he saw that as a drawback. I witnessed my dad fight aging a little and learned I don't want to fight it because I don't have much of a choice. I have an aunt who's 82, full of life, lives on her own and does all kinds of different things with people. When I phone her to say let's go out for dinner, she has to check her schedule! I want to be like that.

I've learned a lot from my parents about getting older: to not put things off, to work towards things that I want to do and to worry less about money. You only get one "kick at the can." My mom and dad owned a nice chunk of land where I grew up and their big dream was that one day, they were going to sell the property. It was worth a good sum of money. They did sell it and three months later my mom got sick with colon cancer, so she didn't get to spend a penny of the money. They put it off and lost in some ways. I learned not to repeat that.

When I was younger I wanted to be this "big person." I wasn't interested in what was going on around me I was more interested in me! As I get older, I don't worry about what people think of me. I can't be out there to please them. We're taught that it sounds selfish, but it's important to me that I please myself first. When I was younger I was trying to pursue happiness whereas now happiness is a by-product of enjoying my life and the people in my life. My perspective now is less about conquering people and the world, and more focused on enjoying friendships and relationships.

THE INVITATION

❧

16

ROSE'S STORY

Rose is a 61-year-old woman of East-Indian origin, an empty nester with three adult children and two grandchildren. Since retiring at the age of 58, she has lived in Toronto and tries to spend the winter in India. Rose is the youngest of five sisters. She volunteers at a women's detox centre, where she does administrative work. She loves travelling, photography, stand-up comedy and spending time with her granddaughters.

Having this conversation with Rose feels as though we are sitting together on a boat cruise, watching the setting sun reflect shades of hot pink on the lake as she travels back and forth in time.

When I think of what my age means to me, I look back and feel I've lived many lives. First was my childhood in Aden, Yemen. I was almost 13 when we moved to India. Then at the age of 17, I went to Abu Dhabi and got a job. When I was 20, I moved to Dubai to work for a large oil company and that's where I met my husband. We got married, had three children and we worked for the same company at different locations for 20 years. I feel I lived my best life during those 20 years.

Then we immigrated to Canada, when we were both 40. When we first arrived, we lived in a house and my children went to nearby schools. But my husband couldn't get a job. I took a junior position and worked my way up again, but he just couldn't find employment. For an Indian man to stay at home while his wife was out working goes completely against the grain. He found it very difficult to accept.

My husband was sad and angry when he was diagnosed with a brain tumour. He was young, just 42 years old, and had been in good health until then. I think he felt indestructible. He was extremely intelligent and accomplished. He worked very hard, seized every opportunity and was the one who decided we should move to Canada. He believed that all the hard work we put in would pay off and we could have an even better life in Canada. Then he got sick and could not believe this could happen to him; he didn't want to die. He didn't want to accept what was happening. He looked for treatments all the time, desperately trying to find a way to survive.

When he was very ill, I was extremely stressed out. My health took a turn for the worse. I became borderline diabetic and my blood pressure started going up. It actually reached the point that when he died I thought I was going to die too. I think it does happen when someone who is very close to you is dying, you feel you're dying too.

During the final year of his life, our family was dealing with trauma and crises, so it was a matter of getting through one day at a time. I went for counselling to help me deal with the situation and the loss. I was very sad that my husband had to suffer the way he did and that his life was cut short, and I was angry at my fate — becoming a widow and feeling like my life was over at the age of 45. Looking back, I can see that I am stronger than I expected myself to be. If someone had told me that when I was 40 living in Dubai, we would immigrate to Canada with three children, and a few years later my husband would become ill and die, I might have dug a hole in the ground and buried myself. I couldn't have imagined dealing with something like that. My husband and I had a partnership, we did everything together, planned together and made financial decisions together. Friends who knew what was going on would say, "I don't know how you come to work, how you're managing, you're so strong," and I'd think to myself, "They don't know that I'm just falling apart."

I thought I would not survive the year after he died. I remember thinking that I had lived such a wonderful life, married a great person, had three beautiful, healthy children, travelled and done everything I wanted to do and more, I was ready to die. If there was a way I could die instead of him, I would have changed places because he wanted to live and I was ready to die. Sometime after he passed away, I came to my senses — I think I had temporarily lost my mind — and I came to see it as God's plan because my children were young and needed their mother. I began a new life as a widow and a single mother.

After their father died, my children felt they couldn't depend on me to be there for them. They saw me going downhill and I said to them, "You guys need to look after each other." I think they were scared that I would die. I remember thinking at that time that I have to live until they come of age and can look after themselves, then they won't need me so much and I can go.

Since then my thinking has changed. I think my children need me to be around as long as possible, and I would like to be there for them as long as I'm healthy. I don't want to be a burden on them. If and when they get married and have kids, I want to be around for that. When my children went to university, I moved to Toronto, and, quite literally, to an empty nest. So now I am an empty-nester with a cat.

I don't see getting older as aging — I see it as living life. I think of every year lived as another year added onto my life. "Okay, I've lived another year, and another year, and another." I look back and evaluate what I have done during that year. I think of "old" as experienced — having lived many years and experienced life more than others. The older you get, the more life experiences you have that young people don't have. It can also be when someone feels they have lived enough and have given up on life. I felt old when I watched my husband's illness age him and saw his life end in front of my eyes.

I feel I was never really young. I started working when I was 17 because of my family's financial situation, so I grew up fast. In my 20s, life felt so busy — working, raising a family, visiting relatives in India every year — that I didn't live in the moment as much as I should have. I had such a wonderful life and now looking back, I feel I didn't appreciate how lucky I was. I took my life for granted.

When I was 57, there were many changes at work that were causing me a lot of stress, and I made the decision to take early retirement. My children had grown up into responsible, independent adults and were doing well. I figured that my health was more important than my finances. After losing their father at an early age, I felt that my children would rather have a parent than for me to have more money. I retired with mixed feelings, though — on the one hand, I was happy to be free of the stress I was experiencing at work, but on the other hand, I regretted having to retire at 58 after working so hard to reach that level since immigrating to Canada.

I'm trying to live in the moment now with more consciousness. I live in a beautiful apartment and have a view of the lake. When I open my eyes in the morning, I see the lake and think how lucky I am to be living here. I wasn't expecting to live alone, but now I've started appreciating all the things I have in my life, rather than focusing on the things that I don't have. My children give me a sense of purpose, and I feel blessed that I have enough for my needs and am able to help others by supporting various charities.

When my mother was dying, she was in India and I was in Dubai. Her deterioration was a natural progression because she had a lot of health problems. I admired her because she had lost her husband, my father, when she was 43 and he was 50. I saw how devastated she was. I think the fact that she lived for 20 years after he died and saw her six children grow up was a great accomplishment. She felt that it was okay to die, she had done what she needed to do and she wanted me to accept the fact that she was going to die. I was the youngest, her baby. I was so afraid of the moment when she would go and leave me. The last time I was with her she told me, "You can't expect me to live forever, with all the health problems I have. You will have to go on living without me." I cry even now when I think of her.

She asked that I not be told that her condition was serious because I believe she felt I could not bear to see her suffering in hospital; she knew how painful that would be for me. She died when I was on the flight to India and when I landed I was told she had passed away. I remember being very nervous about seeing her dead body at the wake. I thought I would not be able to handle that. I was already devastated at losing her; she was a jolly person and had very soft skin. I thought I would find it unbearable to see her in a coffin, her body cold and hard.

I want to start writing about my life so that my grandchildren will know about me. My children did not have grandparents. I look at other people and think some of them have no idea how lucky they are to have grandparents. I saw my only surviving grandparent once when I was 10. We had gone to India on vacation and when I saw her I remember being surprised thinking that she looked like the British children in my school because she was fair-skinned and her hair had turned white. There wasn't much of a connection between us. I was just a 10-year-old kid and she wasn't in good health. I couldn't communicate with her because I didn't speak her language and she didn't speak English, so we just smiled at each other.

I do talk with my children about growing older and sometimes we joke about it. One time I told my kids, "Just put me in a seniors home when I'm old because I don't want to be a burden on you." And sometimes my kids will joke with me, "So that's where you want to go, right? You don't want us to take care of you, you want to go to a nursing home, right?" I know of people living in seniors' residences who are quite happy — they attend organized activities and have people of their own age to interact with. That sounds good to me! For as long as I have my mental capacity, that's what I would like, but if I become senile, I'd like my children to be more involved in my care.

I would like to die with my children near me. I think all of them would be devastated; they're probably hoping to have me around for a long time. But they have seen their father die and experienced a parent's funeral, so maybe they won't take it as badly as I did when my mother passed away. I don't think there's a way to actually prepare my children for my death. Having seen one parent die, they understand the value of having a parent and they treasure it because they know I will die sometime.

Recently I went to the cemetery with my two daughters to visit my husband's grave. We have a joint grave and I said to my daughters, "If I die in India, I don't want you to bring my body back, just bring my ashes and bury them here." My younger daughter just nodded because I think she's not as fearful about my dying, but the older one said, "Can we please not talk about you dying right here at the cemetery?"

Another time, my older daughter and I were talking about the problems my eldest sister is having with her health and that she is thinking about going into a seniors' home. My daughter asked me what I would want for myself, would I like to live in India in a residence with people I am familiar with or to stay here in Canada? That's when I realized that she was actually ready and willing to have this conversation with me. Maybe it's the trauma of what she went through with her father's terminal illness and the thought of going through that again that scares her. I think each of my three children deal with grief and loss differently.

Even though it's almost 15 years since my husband died and 31 years since my mother passed away, I still get emotional when I talk about their passing. The feelings are there, just put aside and when I think about it again, it makes me sad. It takes me right back. I think if you're really close to someone, the feeling of loss never goes away completely, you just put it on the back burner. When I start talking about them, all those emotions come back.

I remember thinking when my husband was dying that I was glad he didn't waste any time — he lived life to the fullest. We didn't wait for retirement to travel, we didn't wait to do anything, we didn't wait until we got older, we did everything when we had the opportunity to do it. You can't waste the years because you don't know how long or short your life is going to be.

❧

17

Varda's Story

Varda was born in Basel, Switzerland. She is a wife, mother, grandmother, performer, teacher, businesswoman, lecturer, lifelong learner, and, at 89 years old, is going strong. She is fluent in seven languages and eloquent in all of them. She has always loved to sing, and was the first person to sing Hebrew and Yiddish songs on Swiss radio. During the Second World War, she sang for Jewish refugees, including a poignant experience singing for a group of children rescued from Bergen-Belsen concentration camp. In 1949, Varda moved to Toronto with her first husband, archeologist Elie Borowski and their 1-year-old son, Zeev. Elie and Varda divorced in the early 1950s. Varda tapped into her resourceful nature: she worked in a factory and ran a rooming house, cooking and cleaning for boarders. She sang for small Jewish communities in Canada, became a music teacher and conducted many choirs over the years. She remains an active and curious person, participating in book clubs, teaching Yiddish and delivering lectures in Toronto and Los Angeles.

The best risk I took in my life was marrying my first husband to get out of Switzerland. It was a big risk. I left secure surroundings and went into the world. I didn't know what was going to happen, but I wanted so badly to get out. I don't know why, I had a feeling. It was too small for me. It was like a golden cage. I already knew that perhaps he was not the man I should marry, but he was the way out of the golden cage, so I took that risk. If I hadn't taken it I would never have known what I have in me. I would have married a nice Swiss guy, been a nice hausfrau and never developed what I have.

It was also the most challenging transition in my life: leaving comfortable surroundings in Switzerland, arriving in a new country with a 10-month-old baby, without much money and facing the challenges. That was unbelievable. I didn't have the language barrier because I spoke English, but everything else was very, very different.

What helped me get through it was my upbringing. I was not a spoiled kid, we were not wealthy, and I saw that my mother had to work when my father died. I grew up in very realistic surroundings. Work was not hard for me and I think that's very important. In Canada, I worked in a factory finishing blouses. I worked double-shifts if I needed to. I am very proud that I could adjust to any situation that I had to face. I wouldn't shy away if I had to be a cleaning lady. It didn't bother me. Even today, if I would have to move into one room, it wouldn't kill me. Not that I would love to, but I could adjust.

Old means experienced. If we are very lucky we become wiser and we should share this wisdom with the younger generation. It is very important to be around young people when you're old. I think it's wonderful. You are forced to keep up with new developments and you see the world around you in a different way.

Having children when you're older keeps you young. I had my son when I was young and, in my second marriage, I had my daughter when I was 41. My mother had me when she was 41 also. It was a wonderful experience because I wanted my daughter so badly. I was much more knowledgeable. When you're young most of the time you have children because it's expected of you, but you don't know what to do with them. But, at 41, I knew exactly what I wanted to do. I'm proud of my children. I had a wonderful son and I have a wonderful daughter. What I'm most proud of is that they were both "menschen." They have a wonderful soul and a wonderful heart. So I'm very proud of that.

My mother came from Switzerland to help me when I divorced, and she helped me bring up my son. She saw it as a new challenge for herself, to have a young grandchild to bring up again. My mother was my role model. She was so interested in everything. She was absolutely current. She read the news to me to make sure that I was properly informed. She was part of the living world. My younger friends didn't care if I was home or not when they came to visit. They were fine with my mother because they could talk to her about everything. She was wise. I have the same experience with my young friends. They would ask, "Varda, can I come over to talk to you?" As long as I can share my knowledge with people, that makes me very happy. I see that they appreciate it. I didn't know that I had that to give. I had no idea that what I have in me people would find interesting.

I'm proud to say my age. I think being comfortable with one's age has to do with culture. In Poland, the culture was not to talk about or say your age. They may not have known their real age or said they were younger or older to get out of the country. In Switzerland, you knew when you were born and were used to telling the truth, including your age. When I arrived in Canada, I had a friend who was 10 years older than me. As the years went by I said to her, "You know, very soon I am going to be older than you; you always lose a few years when you tell your birth date!" It was real, she became younger and I became older. We crossed somewhere and I became older!

I only feel old if my body tells me so. It's the aches and pains that accompany the aging body. What helps me is to be occupied, and then it becomes secondary. I think that's the secret. There are certain illnesses where you can't help it, but if it's just that the knees don't work, that everything hurts in the morning, that it's hard to get around — you cannot let that take over. You have to occupy your brain with something else or your body takes over. I keep myself occupied with many things: teaching the younger generation Yiddish through songs, singing and performing on stage; learning what is current in art, architecture, design, and innovation; researching and preparing lectures and talks.

My head would like to do a lot of things, but my body doesn't allow me, like travelling. It became too difficult. To tell you the truth, if I return to Switzerland, my school friends are not there anymore. They've passed away except for one who is very ill. That's really what the problem is — my friends and the circle I grew up with shrinks every day, every minute, because if they were older than I am, they're not here anymore. It's sad, it's very sad. I try not to be scared. As long as I'm here, I'm going to take advantage of whatever I can do and when it hits me, that's it.

Once I retired, I started to do things that I never had time to do. Some people are amazed when I tell them my age — this is too funny! They tell me, "You shouldn't tell your age, you look much younger!" And I say, no I'm very proud of my age and I want to tell others that there really is no age limit, you can go on and learn and teach for as long as you are alive, as long as the brain works! Inside I feel vibrant and vital. I don't know if it has to do with being on stage and singing. I sang for years, in my late teens and 20s in Switzerland, and then later in Canada, with various Jewish charities, like Keren Kayemeth. In recent years, I sang whenever I gave my talk about the music of Mordechai Gebirtig or about growing up as a Jew in Switzerland. Mostly, I sang Yiddish songs. I love the Yiddish language and these songs bring three of my great loves together: Yiddish, music and singing.

I think perhaps that is what keeps me young. I want to live in "today" and learn whatever I still can. I go to meetings, lectures, the opera. I have new decisions to make every day and I'm not sure how to handle them — every day there is something new to learn. It's amazing — I'm 89 and still learning. It's never too late to learn.

Several years ago, I was attending a talk related to Yiddish and was chatting with the organizer about my interest in the wonderful songs of Mordechai Gebirtig. She encouraged me to give a talk on that subject, and that's how my career as a public speaker began, when I was in my 80s. I gave that talk about Gebirtig in various locations in Toronto, and at the Westside JCC in Los Angeles, where the attendees — elderly Jewish men and women, some American-born, others immigrants from Europe — not only ate up every word, but had tears in their eyes as they heard me sing, and as I encouraged them to sing along to songs many hadn't heard since their own childhoods. It was a deeply moving experience. When I gave my first talk, people were enthusiastic about the things that I spoke about, that I know. They had no idea about the information I gave them, so that makes me feel good. It's a huge contribution. I would like to give a talk about the music of early Zionist songs. We forgot all of that, and these are such wonderful songs of idealism, which I think is missing now, and I want to remember that.

Audiences appreciated that talk so much that they started asking about what else I would talk about. I was thinking about talking about my experiences growing up as a Jew in Switzerland, from 1921 to 1949, that means both pre-war and during the war, what we could do and couldn't do, what we knew and what we didn't know. But I was concerned that the topic would not be of interest to anyone in Canada. I quickly learned that the opposite was true and I gave that talk to a variety of organizations in Toronto and at two well-attended salons held at my daughter's home in Los Angeles.

Now I am researching and writing a new talk about the Righteous Ones in Switzerland (and potentially other countries), the non-Jews who risked their lives to help Jews during WWII. There were a few who never received international accolades, like Schindler, and who were far nobler than him, so I want to bring their stories to light.

I'm always preparing, thinking about something else. These days I am working on preparing lessons for my young friends by teaching Yiddish through songs. That's where we started and then they said, "Hey Varda, it would be nice if we could write." They never went to Hebrew school, so I started to teach them the aleph-beyt and now they're starting to read Hebrew. I'm excited because these people are excited! I'm excited that I can teach them something, and they are excited that they can learn from me.

I think it's important to take care of how you look and not get sloppy about your appearance. I think older people shouldn't let themselves go. Go to the hairdresser, have your hair done, dress properly, put some lipstick on! I welcomed a few visitors into my home, and one was an acquaintance interested in my Yiddish and Hebrew sheet music. I told my friend, who had accompanied the woman — who was well into her 80s — that I didn't understand why this other woman didn't pluck her facial hairs. She might not be able to see them anymore, but everyone else could! I remember what my mama used to say, a lot of the things she used to say I understand now. When I was young, I didn't know what it meant. She would say, "As long as I don't look in the mirror, I do not know how old I am." And that's with me, too. And I'm shortsighted, so I don't see all my wrinkles!

Varda died in January 2013. She was one of the first interviewees to participate in this project. I did not yet ask questions about death and dying, and I wish I had. Her daughter, Rhona, contacted me and generously agreed to share the intimate details of her mother's dying and death.

Rhona's Story (Varda's daughter)

Rhona is a professional life coach, facilitator, and trainer of elementary teachers in a social-emotional learning curriculum. She was born in Toronto and lives in a small town in northern California with her wife, their two kids and a dog.

I'd been in Toronto mid-November and my mother seemed fine. In early December she gave one of her talks to an organization and was having digestive stuff, burping, weird little minor symptoms. She was supposed to leave for Florida and spend January there, but she wasn't feeling 100%. She went to her family doctor, who thought it was just some digestive issues. He gave her something for her stomach and it wasn't really helping.

Then I was in Texas with my kids and my partner, Jen, visiting her family for Christmas. My mum and I were talking on the phone and she said, "You know, I just don't feel great. I think I should just cancel the Florida trip." So then it was the holidays and her doctor was away, everyone was gone. Finally, right after the holidays, my mum goes in for an ultrasound. It was probably January 6, it was the first day she could get in. They see something on her liver, and in fact, my mum wouldn't tell me that.

She called me and said, "Geoff (who was her doctor and also an old family friend) wants to talk to you."

"What's wrong?"

"Talk to Geoff."

So I speak to him and he says, "There's something on her liver. I need to get her in for a test. I'm going to try and get her in as quickly as possible."

I said, "Can you give me as much of a heads-up as possible? I will get on a plane."

Within two days my mother went in for the test and they found cancer. She was cancer-ridden. The fact that she only had a little bit of digestive discomfort was crazy. It was in her liver. It was in her stomach. It was in her colon. We realized it probably started in her gallbladder. It was everywhere. Everywhere. Lymph nodes. Everything. The fact that she did not have major symptoms was a miracle.

My mum could be a tough cookie. She was strong in so many ways and powered through. She had a real work ethic and life ethic, "You don't complain."

She was an incredibly passionate person and had a lot of hobbies and interests that were vibrant: politics, music, singing, art, design, innovation. There are some people who get old; my mother never got old. There was an incredible youthfulness and zest that remained very present in her until the end. She was unstoppable until she wasn't, and then she died. There was no fear of death. I don't think grace, dealing with things with grace, is a word I would have ever used for her. But what stands out was that my mother dealt with death with grace. She was calm, loving, expressive, gentle, funny. She had so much gallows humour. It was great.

We immediately went to the financial guy. We immediately went to the attorney. It was three weeks from diagnosis to death. For the first week to a week and a half, she was still okay. It was such a gift. She was still pretty much okay. The last week and a half — no.

We talked a lot about gifts — financial gifts, tangible gifts. It was January, so a lot of her friends were in Florida and she didn't get to see many of them, but she spoke to people, emailed with people. The friends who were able to see her — those were some of the beautiful moments. I got to hear her speaking with the people who she gave gifts to, and a couple of really generous monetary gifts.

In both cases with the two people they said, "No, no, no, no. You can't do this. I don't want to do this now."

She said, "I can. You need to let me. I want to give this to you with warm hands, not cold."

I remember our friends, Violette and Norman. Both of them were very close to my mum. I remember my mother telling them as they were saying goodbye how much they meant to her, what wonderful people she thinks they are, how much the friendship has meant, and it was just so beautiful, so exquisite. It was exquisite and I don't think my mum was that person for so much of her life. She had such a hard shell, could be so tough with people. She rose to the occasion of her death, and gave many gifts to people, emotional and tangible, and that was something.

Our close family friend, Jennie, flew in from Vancouver to see my mum. I remember we were sitting on my mum's bed and that this was an incredible opportunity to talk about it.

So we asked her, "If you had advice from this perspective, what would you say to us?"

She said, "Don't care so much what other people think, and I am someone whom other people looked at and think I haven't cared. I left Switzerland, I divorced, I separated from my second husband, I was a singer, I did all these things that you'd think I didn't care what other people thought. And I still cared. I wish I hadn't cared so much."

That was her big thing. Don't care so much what people think. I remember that a lot.

She died at home; we never took her anywhere. Her doctor was willing to do whatever was needed to help her die at home comfortably. We had to move her from her regular bed to a hospital bed a few days before she died. She was on a lot of morphine. She couldn't get up at that point. It was awful, my mother was such a dignified, elegant person and her bowels, things were going through her and it was awful. That was awful for her. It was so humiliating, that was really painful.

I remember we were trying to lift her up in the sheets and blankets so she could be supported and move her onto the hospital bed. There were five or six of us — family and friends — around her. My mum looks up at all of us and says, "You know, this is the last time you're going to push me around." I looked at her and said, "Mummy, I think this is the first time!" It was like that, and that was in the space. She laughed, she thought that was funny, "You're probably right!"

This was my mother's relationship with death. I don't think she was ever afraid of death since losing my brother. He was 24, so my mum was a year younger than I am now when my brother died. God, I hadn't thought about that either, that she was this age when he died. After losing him, death was not a frightening thing. She probably wished she were dead. For a long time she didn't believe there was anything else. But then I think my spirituality and some of my weird woo-woo experiences had a profound impact on her. My mother was very curious the last few years of her life about the stuff that I was experiencing and sharing with her around a spiritual connection. She was hopeful that she'd see my brother again, that she'd see my dad, some of her friends, her siblings, because there were so few people who were alive.

She was very adamant about minimizing any physical distress. She did not want to linger, even if it meant medicating her up the wazoo and not being conscious. The distress she had was about me, not about her. She knew I would feel such pain to lose her. We spoke on the phone every day — my mother drove me nuts and I adored her! Both were true. She would drive me nuts if she was coming to visit now, but I wish she could come visit now! I miss talking to her. I miss her every day. That hasn't changed much in the two years since she died, and that surprises me.

I always assumed I'd be with her when she died. But she wouldn't die with me in the room. She just wouldn't. I would speak and she would turn toward my voice. I think we were so connected that she would hear me or know I was there, and then want to be there, want to be present with me. So I had to make the decision to leave. My wife, Jen, and my mum's best friend, Tal, were with her when she died, and I wasn't.

An epiphany for me was that I spent a lot of time both when she was still conscious, and then unconscious, at her bedside saying, "It's okay

Mummy, you can go, I'm okay," and I realized I was lying through my teeth. I was so full of shit. I didn't really feel it. It wasn't okay for her to go. I mean she had to go and I had to let her go, but it wasn't okay. Wow! It would have been really mature of me to believe what I was saying! You're going, but I'm not okay with it! She probably knew that and it's why I had to leave the room.

My mum always said that she wanted to die in her sleep, so when this illness happened she said, "You know, maybe this is really the idea." I think given the choice, instead of a week and a half of discomfort, she would have had a day. But in the end she would have said this is a really good way to die. It was quite extraordinary. I think she was extraordinary.

There were a couple of times when my mum looked at me with such pure, unadulterated, unconditional love that it took my breath away. I always knew my mother loved me, it's not like I doubted her love, but there was always so much judgment attached. I got to see her look at me without an iota of judgment, just this pure almost child-like love. So I had a very special experience with her dying. I feel very grateful.

I would truly aspire to be like that. Of course I would aspire to be more like that before dying, right? But yes, my mother was very inspiring. I feel very inspired by how she was when she died. My mother taught me that death is an opportunity. If you know you're going to die (which, in truth, we all do!) death is an opportunity. Death is an opportunity to express love, to get greater clarity about what is important and to really be who you are.

≈

18

Maggie's Story

Maggie is 64 years old, a teacher of young children and their families, a Kundalini Yoga teacher, an artist and a community person. The most important people in her life are her husband of 38 years, her three children, Ali, Zoe and Piper ("my sun, my moon and my star"), her sister, who "even though we don't always agree, she lets me say what I need to even though she says something different" and her friend, Heather, who has known her for all her adult life. Maggie loves wearing plaids and tartans, and cooking with the TV on.

I never really heard my parents talk much about growing older. My mother only lived until age 55. She was pretty young when she died. My father was in the hospital after suffering a stroke at the same time as my mother was dying; they were at different ends of the hospital floor. He pulled through; she did not. He lived the last ten years of his life having to deal with paralysis and died in his 70s.

It sounds ridiculous, but my sister and I had no idea that my mother was dying. Knowing what I know now, I can see that I was blind. But my mother was full of grace and wisdom until the end. She allowed me to help her, to be engaged with her sickness a little bit, but she never talked about it. I never knew when she was in pain. She was — I don't like to use the word — like a martyr. We didn't know she was dying because we were naive and, I don't know, I didn't think my mother would die. Why?

MAGGIE'S STORY

Both my sister and I didn't think about it and my mom didn't talk about it. You didn't talk about it in those days. Nobody talked about death. It's ridiculous, it would have prepared us a lot if we had known how to deal with death.

We did not understand what was happening. There were four of us children at home: my sister Mary was 21, I was 19, my brother Jim was 18 and my brother David was 15. We were pretty young. We were taking care of my dad who had had a stroke. We didn't know how to take care of ourselves, let alone our ill dad. We were not equipped. We should have had social workers. If it happened today there would be groups for us, someone would have come and said, "Now do you know what to do with this and that?" We were given the responsibility of making sure my father kept his appointments, took his pills and kept to his strict diet.

Then three months later, I was diagnosed with Hodgkin's Lymphoma Disease. There I was in my 20s, my mom had died, my father had had a stroke, and I had cancer. When I got really sick with cancer, it seemed that everything was out of control. I was so worn out. I was going to school at night, I was working full time, taking care of my dad. I felt quite alone. I was out of sync with my peers, with my friends. Who has cancer? Who has a parent who's dying? Now everybody's parents are dying, but not then. I couldn't really ask for support from my own family because they were in their own chaos. But you know, it happens to everybody, for some people it happens younger. I didn't know whether I was going to make it, whether I was going to live or die, so I faced that at a very young age. I remember thinking, "My purpose isn't over." I believed I had to have children, it was like, "I can't die until I have children." In a way I'm very grateful because it set me up with a lot of empathy for others. I'm not afraid to be with people who are dying. I'm not afraid of a lot of things because of it.

I learned that dying and death are a process. Some people do it with full consciousness and others are unable to, and if you can assist someone to have some kind of consciousness or peace or contentment, it's a great gift. You want to walk with those who are dying as much as those who are living.

I've had a few friends who have died. There was one particular woman who had multiple sclerosis and a whole group of us took care of her. Every three hours we would rotate, she let us be there with her, on her journey, and each of us had a role. Each of us could engage in a different way. She knew what we could do and what we could not do, like I did not help with the bathing part, I helped with feeding her when she switched to having liquid nourishment through a tube. So I thought, "Wow! If somebody has that understanding of how to die, what a gift!" Because you can bring people into it — we were in it together even though it was her process.

I had another friend who died of cancer, and somehow I'd made an agreement to be there if she needed me when she was dying. For whatever reason I ended up there, the only one. Everyone had gone home and I was with her as she died. I think it was a gift for me to be there because when she went unconscious, I said, "Let go. I'm here. I'm going to stay here." And I remember thinking, what an amazing gift that she let me be there for such an intimate part of her life.

Both deaths taught me a lot because I hadn't been there for my mother. My father had decided that we should all go home that night. He had a hard time losing her; he didn't want to be there. I wanted to stay, and I was always annoyed and sad that I didn't stay. My friend let me be there, and it's remarkable to me that I got to be there to support her. It was a way for me to put closure on that part of my mum's death. I want somebody to be there to support me when it's my time, to say, "It's okay, go."

I've also learned that energy, and what you do with it, is very important. We can freak out, or try to maintain our energy with some kind of stability. We can give it to each other and we can take it in too, sometimes negatively. We are really tied to each other, all of us, and with our children. We have to be more conscious of the energetic connections that we make. We have those exchanges all the time, but we're just not always aware of it. When we are dying, we can also draw energy from the people who are caring for us. I know what that feels like; I've felt it. As long as people are in agreement, it's okay to use it. It's a great thing, a great healing thing.

I don't fear death or dying. I think of death as just another step. I believe there's something after death so do your best now and the after will be something else. I do say I'm not coming back this way — I'm coming back better! Probably the thing I'm afraid of the most is being alone, not having people to talk to.

Before my mother died, she started giving things away; they weren't very valuable things. I didn't really know she was dying. They meant a lot to me — the gifts — and there was more behind the gifts. It wasn't a whole big thing, she'd just say, "I'd like you to have this." I've thought recently about what I'd like to give away. I would like to have it organized: give away the things I want to give, do the things I want to do, say the things I want to say now, not when I can't.

I think a lot of who I am is because of my mom. She was a great hero to me. Her presence was a huge loss. She, in her own straitlaced way, was always trying to do new things. She took up sewing when I was in high school and made us clothes, or she took up knitting and made us mittens. But it was always later because she had quite a few kids to take care of, so she was always a little late, like a late bloomer. I feel sometimes that I'm a late bloomer, and that it's okay to keep blooming.

I didn't really learn about aging. That was probably the problem — there weren't a lot of influences around me. I didn't have a lot of relationships with old people. Two people who did inspire me were my two great-aunts, Big Mary and Essie. My great-aunts never married and they lived together most of their lives. Every year my parents went together on holiday to Europe to visit my father's mother in Scotland, and Big Mary and Essie would be our babysitters. We were four siblings and they were responsible for looking after all of us. They hadn't had children, so their expectations of us were different from my parents'.

It was the late 1950s and they'd arrive at our house with brown bags filled with bubble gum. During the two weeks my parents were away, we received bubble gum at least three times a day. Firstly in the morning we'd find our bubble gum waiting for us on the table at the place where each of us sat for breakfast. Then again at supper there would be bubble gum, and any time we would set off to do something, there would be bubble gum waiting for us. It was such a treat! They must have had hundreds of pieces with them because we received some every day.

These two grey-haired women, in their late 60s, were typical old-fashioned ladies with their brown oxford shoes, blue hair and traditional older women's clothes, but they fit no stereotype. They were our "fun" great-aunts. They found a way into our hearts with the gum and the ghost stories Big Mary told. They challenged the image of what older women then were expected to be and do. They were two women who showed me another path.

When I was about 54, I did some studying about aging in the shamanic teachings. According to them, when you turn 54 you are much like a 27-year-old. You're starting another beginning. At 27, you're usually starting your career or family, and at 54 a new beginning starts again. I interpreted it as an opportunity to start something again. I was either going to stay comfortable or I could do things that would make me stretch, make me feel uncomfortable, but in the end would benefit me as I grew older.

After having cancer in my 20s, I had post-traumatic stress disorder about my health for years. I haven't had any health problems — touch wood — since then. I'm on no medications. I try to eat well; I'm a vegetarian. I wasn't born with athletics in my life; I've had to learn to do it. When the kids were little I didn't do much, then in my 50s I started to jog, and I jogged for 10 years. I don't do it anymore, but I realized that my body needs to do something in order to stay healthy. Now I spin twice a week, and I see a personal trainer with three other women once a week. My husband and I snowshoe and kayak quite a bit. I could not bear to be the person not doing anything, and I'm kind of privileged too because I can do it. There are a lot of women who can't.

I do notice a certain invisibility that comes with age. I might be walking down the street and no one looks at me. The other thing that's happened is that I'm offered a seat on the bus sometimes, which kind of freaks me out because I feel very able-bodied, but I'm grey-haired. I've never dyed my hair, so right away you know I'm an older person. That's been a dilemma. I've often thought, "Maybe if I dye my hair…" and my kids say, "No!" They love my hair! They don't think I need to. My daughters don't dye their hair either.

I think there are young people who are readily open to people of different ages in society, and older people who can be very judgmental about younger people: young people are supposed to be quiet, not supposed to talk or have much to say. And I love that my kids have so much to say! They've taught me a lot! I think you have to keep it open both ways.

In my late 50s, I started to train as a yoga teacher and almost everyone in the class was 20 to 25 years younger. I didn't say, "I can't do it because I'm in my late 50s." I knew I was going to do it no matter what. I chose yoga because I saw myself doing it at 80, I thought it would benefit me and it would benefit others. I always felt that yoga should be for everybody and that as a yoga teacher, I should be able to teach anybody. I never in a million years thought I would be teaching yoga to the elderly. It just fell into my hands. The instructor was away and now I have all these classes. The money that was given to this community centre was given by an elderly woman who could not find a yoga class. Apparently yoga for seniors is in high demand, so there can be up to 20 people in a class. My favourite student is a little blind lady; everyone said she did not know what she was doing. She does not do much, she's quite wizened and I don't think she speaks English that well, but she is doing yoga and her husband is across the room. They are very cute, smiling at each other. She can't see me, but she looks over, expectantly. What's interesting too is that men are participating. I think in the younger age groups, there are more women doing yoga. So what does that say about our culture, that it's suddenly okay to do yoga when you're an older man?

As older people we can provide those things because we have been around. Connectedness is important; we need to connect. And if yoga is a way, I'm happy with that. It's a challenge for me; I have to really step up to the plate. I think I'm being called to do this, and it's hard work! It's like when I was a new schoolteacher in my 20s, I'm a beginner again. I'm looking into where to get more yoga training for seniors because I see myself doing it for the rest of my life, really, if I want to.

I'd like to do more work for others. I started this project called "We Care With Underwear," for the dignity, femininity and hygiene of women in crisis around the world. It began when I was at a fundraiser a few years ago and I asked a woman and her husband how I could help in Haiti. She said, "Collect underwear," and I pooh-poohed it, I didn't want to do that. But I started to collect and got everybody to collect underwear. I went to Haiti and handed it out with my colleague. We visited tent cities and handed out two pairs to every woman, and the impact of that on women was incredible, I mean we nearly caused riots!

Then I connected with a woman from Zimbabwe to help women there who are in prison and were only receiving one pad a day. The discussion became about menstrual pads and I thought, "Hey I can do that." So I've started making menstrual-pad kits, so the women have simple instructions and all the tools needed to make them themselves. Then a friend of my daughter's, who works with street women and prostitutes, asked for underwear, so we sent collected underwear to them. It's all inter-connected.

This new cause found me and I can involve my community. I'm never alone and it's never about me. When I make it about me, I lose the thread. I never identify it as my project, it's "We Care's project." It's about people who are doing it for others who can't do it. It could be us. We just happen to be in a position where we can do it. The more we make it about ourselves, the more we miss. That's just ego. Ego loves to tell us all kinds of stuff. Sure, I fall into self-pity or self-importance. My journey has been a lot of self-pity, so I say to myself, "Get over yourself, who cares?" It's not about me and as soon as I adjust myself, things do open. I think it's a spiritual journey and that it's the journey of your core. It doesn't have to be religious. The minute you open to that way of being, your life will flow.

Maggie died in November 2016. She approved the final edits to her story in February 2016, and I asked to meet her in person. We met at the beginning of March in one of her favourite cafés, up the street from her home. She had just returned from a visit to India with her husband and was full of life and gratitude. I told her it felt like an internet date because up until then we had only connected online. Also, I felt like I was meeting a dear friend. She and I had conversations that you don't normally have with people you just meet, and her love and loveliness shone through her words. We parted that day with a deep embrace, and the next time we would connect was at her Irish, kundalini yoga, shamanic wake.

THE INVITATION

19

Edna's Story

Edna was born in Oklahoma and lives in Ithaca, New York. She is a 50-year-old social worker, and a recently separated mother to 14- and 12-year-old daughters. She lost her mother in the fall of 2011. She likes to read, sing folk music and volunteer at her local hospice. She enjoys getting to know a broad age-range of people through her faith community.

I just turned 50, so I've been thinking more about aging. I think my parents and grandparents set some good models for me, and some poor models for me. My maternal grandparents were not well educated, they didn't go to college, but they worked hard and when they retired, they got in an RV (recreational vehicle), drove out West and moved to Arizona. They seemed to have a fun old age, which is pretty cool.

They were quite old when they died — my grandmother was 79 and my grandfather was 81. I was 25 when they died, and I know this because that year I lost my father and a high school friend who had cancer. My grandmother died, and my grandfather followed her six months later. Within a six-month period, I had those four losses. That was interesting! The very positive thing that came out of it was that I had a closer bond with my mother. I was finally an adult — I was on my own, I was out of college and working, I was married — and because both her parents died one after the other, we ended up talking a lot and bonding over that. My first marriage was ending in divorce that year too, so I was talking to a counsellor. I was fortunate to have lots of good friends in my life and worked through some of it with them. That year gave me the sense of being grateful for today, and of not knowing when it's going to be your turn. I mean there was my 25-year-old high school friend dying that year, as well as my 81-year-old grandparent, so yeah.

My father lived till he was 60; he had a stroke or heart attack and died quite suddenly. He was described as a type-A personality — very high-strung, driven to work hard, a perfectionist — and he didn't have a lot of fun in his life! He worked at his job, then he'd come home and work on our farm or run some cattle. He retired early and died within a couple of years. When he retired, he went with his second wife to do some missionary work in Zambia for 15 months. So I would say that he didn't actually retire, he was someone who very much worked all the time. We think that what brought on his stroke or heart attack was that he'd been out fighting a brush fire on his land that had re-ignited, so there was some stress that day he'd died. He was a "more stress" person.

My maternal grandmother was a great role model. We have a video from the 1970s of her dressing up as a hooker in a black lace body stocking. She was really playful, even as she aged. I would look though Cosmopolitan magazine and she would look at it with me. At the back of the magazine there were advertisements for belly button jewelry, and she'd say, "Let's get some of those!"

There are people who are breaking cultural rules about how to age in my town, Ithaca, which is a liberal, activist community. There are many wonderful role models from the Unitarian Methodist Church, which tends to attract activists and freethinkers. The community is a really accepting place. I see women walking around with grey hair in a braid to their waist and I like that! I also love this community because I have children and we don't live near their grandparents, which limits our connections with older people. When I was in my early 30s, I went to a church retreat and there was a woman who was 75 years old. I walked with her from an outdoor art exhibit back to our retreat. It was about two miles, and I could barely keep up with her! It was just amazing and I remember thinking, "Wow! I want to be like her when I'm in my 70s! I want some 30-year-old to work really hard to keep up with me when I'm walking!"

One special friend I met through my church died at age 95. She was well educated and well travelled. In her final years, she didn't see well, but she was the best-read person that I knew because she received books and news magazines on tape from the society for the blind. So she didn't sit around and deteriorate, she listened to the news and heard the latest novels. She was a great inspiration on how to keep your mind alert, active and engaged.

I don't think there is one age when people are old. My mother was old when she was young, and by that I mean she had an older mindset. She sometimes let her chronological age keep her from doing things. She believed, "I'm old, so I don't this." One of her beliefs was, "If you have children and you're old, you don't grow your hair long. You cut your hair." She felt there were rules about how you should dress, act and look depending on your age. On the other hand, my mom was also a rule breaker! When she was 40, she went back to school and got her nursing degree, and she divorced my dad after 30 years, which was kind of taboo in our Christian community.

I tend to surround myself with people I admire, who age the way I want to age. I'm learning that if you keep active, you'll be able to stay active. Recently I went to play music for a fundraiser to keep companies from storing liquid petroleum, and one of the people collecting the money was Martha, a 90-year-old woman from my church. She'd driven over partially snow-covered roads with another church member and they were handing out information about this cause while I played music! Martha joined people of all ages and backgrounds to protest, and was arrested for picketing. She is someone whom I really admire, as well as her husband who had gone cross-country skiing the day he died. That's how I want to end my life: he went out skiing, he had lunch, he lay down for a nap and then it was over. And she's going strong at 90. She has outlived her husband by quite a few years and she hasn't lost her will to live, whereas my grandfather died six months after my grandma, which I think sometimes happens with older people, after they lose their partner, they lose their will to live.

The times when I feel old now are when I'm around someone who's in their 20s. When I was 25 I felt some pressure; that was a pivotal time in my life. A co-worker is turning 25 soon and I said to her, "Oh I hope you don't feel like I felt then, that a quarter century had passed and what had I done with my life?" I also realized, "Oh wow, I could be her mother! In a couple of years I could be someone's grandmother!" That can make me feel old.

When I was 27, I worked at a Fortune 500 company where I was doing very well and making a good salary but I hated the job, just hated it. I'd cry when I got up before going to work; I'd cry when I came home in the evening. I thought, "My life is too short to do things I don't enjoy." So I left that job and I went into the Peace Corps. Not only was it a transition from highly paid work to volunteering, but it was a tough transition from living in American to living in African culture. I had to do with much less than what I'd been used to — I didn't have hot water, I didn't have electricity in my house for seven months, I had to walk or wait for a bus for a very long time, or ride a bike to get places. I had to adjust to that culture and the loneliness involved with that. I valued the chance to live somewhere else and to learn a different language. We were taught in our classes about the culture and that the elders were to be respected. There were even words in their languages that were reserved for the elderly. "Mzee" meant Elder, so if you saw an elderly man, you would greet him with "Mzee," even though you didn't know him.

I'd left this high-powered, high-paid job, and in Kenya I saw people who were pretty happy without a lot and I thought, "Oh wow!" I didn't believe that money was key and here was a country full of people showing me that I was right. There was much more of a sense of living day-to-day and living in the present, rather than in the future. I just loved the experience. I felt that I learned about myself, being there alone. When you're by yourself, you learn about yourself, and that definitely happened.

I really felt called to be involved in hospice work. My mother had been a nurse, and she knew about hospice and had informed me. I'd also heard about it through my faith community and older church members. I knew some people who were in the hospice and when I visited them, I saw how helpful it was for them. So I became a volunteer and I have spent time with a couple of people who were dying. The beauty of hospice, as I've experienced it, is that they let people work through the process of dying and they also provide pain relief and anxiety relief. I see how people are fearful of death, so it's helpful if you can learn more about it, and have it not be so scary. I don't want to be in pain when I die. I don't want to be anxious when I die. I know that some of the end processes of dying cause some anxiety: your body's systems are shutting down and it can be hard to catch your breath, and that's anxiety-producing.

It was interesting for me to be present with someone who was dying, and to know that just being there was enough. Sometimes it was to allow family members to go and run errands and not have to worry about their relative. Often I would just sit there and breathe and meditate with the dying person. Sometimes I would practice Tonglen, the loving-kindness meditation, breathing in their pain or anxiety or fear or discomfort, and breathing out inner peace. So it was as helpful to me as it was to them and their family members.

I think American culture, western culture, hasn't really embraced the concept of dying well, so often death isn't talked about, it isn't planned for, and death isn't in any way positive for people. A friend's husband was dying of liver cancer and she called me in the middle of the night when she went to the hospital, probably also because I am a social worker, and I joined her. I don't think the doctor told them how close he was to the end and they were unprepared. It was a really big shock. Looking back, I wonder why I didn't more strongly suggest hospice care and help them get connected. I feel that it's something I'd like to help other people with, whether it's the person dying or their family. I want it to be a natural and supported process for me and my family members.

My mother passed away at age 82. I'm the fourth of five siblings, and my sister had my mother live with her for her last six years. We all talked with my mother about what should happen. She wanted to go to the nursing home. That was her wish. She had been the Director of Nursing in that nursing home years before, she knew people there who were caring for others, and she felt that people would be there for her, and they were.

She was very confident about her religious beliefs and an afterlife, so I felt that she was resolved about her spiritual self. But even though she was a nurse, the dying part was difficult for her. I think what she experienced, what a lot of people experience at the end of life, is anxiety. I don't think they were treating the anxiety, that's why she was having a hard time letting go. My mother would become anxious, and staff at the nursing home would ask her if she wanted to go to hospital and she'd say, "Yes, yes, take me!" Instead they could have said, "You know, this is natural, we're going to help you out, we're going to give you this." I asked my sister to get the hospice connected with her. They did come in and gave her lots of support, but I wish I could have been there.

In truth, maybe I'm projecting some of what I would want onto my mother, like to die at home or to not die in a hospital. But she was a nurse, and she died in a hospital where she did the majority of her nursing, so maybe that was preferable to her. Interesting, I don't know if I had this conversation with her. I know from my sister that she didn't want to die at my sister's home. One of my mother's rules was, "I don't want to die in your house. That will be messy for you, that will be uncomfortable. Will you want to use that room again?" I think she had those feelings because of her cultural upbringing, whereas I think the most beautiful thing that could happen is to die in your own bed, surrounded by your family. My mother may have felt more comfortable being in the hospital — she didn't ask to go back home or to the nursing home to die, so maybe she did make her choice. She had all of us five siblings there with her for American Thanksgiving, which falls on Thursday. We were there until Saturday and she died Sunday morning. Whether she chose to consciously let go then or whether unconsciously she was just able to — she had seen her children and business had been wrapped up.

The following Saturday, we had the memorial service for her. I think some people hate funerals, hate the whole process of losing and mourning someone they love. But we really did celebrate her; we played the songs she wanted, we read scripture that she wanted, I read a poem that was meaningful to me about my mother. Then we passed the microphone around and people told stories, they talked about meeting her or how they became friends, or how they raised children together. It was really beautiful.

It's interesting that I feared my mother dying, but once it happened it felt natural and I was more accepting of it. I don't know why that was, maybe it was just anxiety about losing her. I'm sad and I miss her, but that's okay, it's the natural course of our lives. I don't believe in an afterlife, but I do believe that my mother lives on in me and that I will live on in my children and my friends.

I don't think everyone gets a chance to say goodbye to someone like that, in a public way. So I hope I get that too, naturally. My husband and I are separating, but I have given my best friend directions about what I want — to connect me with hospice should I be too ill or unable to do it myself, what type of spiritual service and memorial there should be — if something happens to me. I know people will be sad, but I want them to celebrate their connection with me.

What I'm hoping is that as I die, I'll be aware and learn something about the transition to not being alive anymore. I probably fear dying more than death. With death when it's done, it's done. Death is an immediate thing. When your body stops, it stops. Life can be short, so we should be doing those things that bring us joy and that we want to do, regardless of our age, because we don't know when it's going to end. I've learned that we're not guaranteed a tomorrow, so follow your heart with work, with relationships, with where you want to live. I didn't know when I was younger that I have so much to be grateful for. I don't think I was ungrateful then, but now I'm more aware of the fragility of life. I've lost people who are my age. I know that life is short and I should be doing what my heart tells me to do because I don't know how much time I'm going to have.

THE INVITATION

❧

20

THE STORY ABOUT JOHN
OR
I KILLED A MAN

On April 2, 2013, I received an email from a friend of a friend saying that his grandfather was interested in the interview project. "I asked my grandfather, who is almost 97, and he is up for it, except the phone is too difficult for him to manage. He has trouble with his hearing. He said, 'Email would be easier for me to write my answers.' Pretty fantastic, eh!"

It certainly was pretty fantastic. I emailed John the next day and included the interview questions. He replied immediately.

Dear Ruth,
The answers to your questions will take much time, and at my advanced age I have become rather slow and irregular. But I will do my best. Tell me, how fast do you want my answers? Then I will try to act on your time schedule.
John

I replied that he could take as long as he needed, not to rush and to answer only the questions he wanted to answer. On April 26, I received this email from his grandson, "I am just writing to ask you if my grandfather ever did an interview with you? I ask because sadly he passed away this week. I was curious if by chance you have some of his final thoughts on getting older. It would be nice to have a copy, if you do.

THE STORY ABOUT JOHN

Thank you."

John died three weeks after I sent him the questions about aging, death and dying. I remember thinking, "I killed him! I killed John! I killed him with these questions about aging and death and dying! The questions stressed his heart, they killed him!" Then I thought some more. He was almost 97. I doubt he would have reached his 90s if questions could have killed him.

But it taught me that I was not immune to the fears about asking these questions, still. Still after three years of interviews, still after asking these questions to dozens of people. Still the superstition lurked somewhere inside me that by talking about death, it will bring death on. I experienced what keeps many of us from asking those questions.

But it was his grandson's request, to know if his grandfather had shared his final thoughts about getting older, that really struck me. His grandson wanted to know what his grandfather would say. His family will never know what John thought about aging or dying or death, or what he knew at 97 that he didn't know when he was a young man.

I invite you to read the chapter with the interview questions. Ask them of yourself, ask your relatives. Before you run out of time, and it's too late to discover the answers.

THE INVITATION

21

YOUR INVITATION: THE QUESTIONS

Dear Reader,

And now, here is your invitation. I respectfully extend it to you and hope you will consider your answers to the interview questions. My wish for you is that you choose those that intrigue you, as well as the ones that scare you a little. Write them down on the blank pages in this chapter or in your personal notebook. You might want to simply "be" with them, let them live with you for a while. Jot down whatever comes up for you — some of it might be familiar and some might surprise you. Or maybe you want to explore without words — through images, the arts, music, movement, or some other way that is appealing to you. There are many ways into these questions, and into your answers. Finding what works for you is part of the process.

These are the interview questions:
1. What are your thoughts and ideas about aging and getting older? What does "old" mean to you?
2. Do you feel comfortable saying your age? What situations make you more or less comfortable sharing your age? What event(s) in your life made you aware of your age, or of getting older?
3. What is the age when people are old? When have you felt "old"?
4. What have you learned from your parents about aging and

YOUR INVITATION: THE QUESTIONS

growing older? (For example, observing their aging process, and their attitudes towards getting older.)
5. From where else did you learn about aging? (For example, television and film, advertising, celebrity, magazines, your culture, relatives, peers, friends, colleagues, role models, etc.)
6. Do you fear aging? What is it that you fear about it?
7. How has your work/career been affected by aging?
8. What are your thoughts about aging and relationships, romance and sex?
9. What changes are you anticipating or expecting, as you get older?
10. Do you prepare yourself for getting older? How?
11. Have you experienced ageism or age-related stigma? What do you think will help address or decrease ageism?
12. What do you know today, at your age, that you didn't know when you were a young/middle-aged adult? What do you appreciate now that you didn't appreciate when you were younger?
13. What are the best things about aging, getting older? What have you gained from your years of living?
14. What are the worst/hardest things about getting older?
15. What are your thoughts and/or experiences with death?
16. What are your thoughts and/or experiences with dying?
17. What do you fear more — dying or death? What do you fear about it?
18. Whose death do you fear more — your own or someone close to you?
19. How would you like to die?
20. Are you preparing yourself for dying and death? How?
21. If you were to share a piece of advice about the experience of aging to help other people grow older, what would it be?

Listed below are the questions I wish I had asked. I didn't have the personal life (or death) experience to know to ask them. Now that I do, I want to share them with you. These questions dig deeper into dying, death and grief.

1. Do you want someone to be there with you when you are dying, or as you die?
2. How are your ideas of death different from 10 or 20 years ago?
3. What did your family teach you about dying, and about death?
4. What hauntings did you have after someone you loved died — during their dying process, as they died, after they died?
5. Did you experience any dreams or visits from the person who died? What happened?
6. What did your family/parents teach you about grieving and mourning? How did they grieve?
7. When in your life have you grieved? When was grief most intense for you?
8. How did you experience grief?
9. What ways did you grieve that were helpful? What did not help you?
10. Did you experience a fog of grief? What happened to you during that time? Looking back, are there any incidents that stand out?
11. What happened to your relationships (spouse, relatives, friendships) while you were grieving?

And now, do you have any other questions? Maybe, while going through the questions, another question surfaced that you want to explore and understand about aging, dying, death or grief.

If you want to, and I do encourage you, ask these questions of the people you love, especially the elders in your life. Extend the invitation to them. I can almost promise you that this conversation will be one you both remember. You will probably learn about yourself in the process and connect with your loved ones in a new way.

Here are some ideas and tips for having these conversations with others:
- Invite one member of your family to share their thoughts about these questions. Clarify if there are any questions they would prefer not to be asked.

YOUR INVITATION: THE QUESTIONS

- Invite one or two members of your family together to discuss a couple of the questions. Decide which question(s) together ahead of time so that everyone has time to think about it.
- Invite your child(ren) or children in your family to discuss one (or more) of the questions.
- Invite one of your elders to share their thoughts with you on as many questions as they feel comfortable.
- Invite a few close friends together for a conversation circle. Decide ahead of time which question(s) you will discuss. You might consider meeting regularly.
- If they agree, you might want to audio or video-record it. You might choose to transcribe it later; it does take a lot of time, but it is worthwhile. It is wonderful to hear and read everyone's thoughts and comments, the stories and humour, the love, and emotion.

Let's continue to grow this list of questions and invite each other to talk about our experiences with aging, dying, death and grief. Let's face this taboo together so that we can understand it and end the silence around it.

Your Notes

YOUR NOTES

THE INVITATION

Acknowledgements

Immense gratitude to the participants and their families. It is because of their courage and generosity that the interview project and this book are realized. They are the following:

Varda Berenstein and Rhona Berens, Edna S. Brown, Jane Christie, Joanne Danby, Doug, Mariana Rolanda Grinblat, Gabriele Hardt, Maggie Thomson Hayes, Emily Johnson, Sylvia Laale, Bradley Lang, Courtney Lawrence, David John Lawrence, Marie, Lucy Richards, and Joel Ulster.

Thanks to my two editors, Brittany Smith and Sarah MacKinnon, who held the integrity of each person's voice while polishing their words and the flow of their story.

Deep bow to my writing coach, Chris Kay Fraser, who helped me sort through the interviews and chaotic threads of this project until I discovered the book that was to be created. She encouraged me to write as my dad died and afterwards, when my grief was fresh, and in the process I found my writing voice and the courage to share it with others.

Heart-felt thanks to dear friends who showed up with so much support and encouragement: Amy Greenleaf Brassert, Hester Dunlap, Krista Ellis, Patricia Gaviria, Tessa Mintz, and Danette Relic.

To Judith Kanee for her love, caring, and compassion during these

ACKNOWLEDGEMENTS

years of losses and transitions, checking in countless times to see how the book was coming along and, more importantly, how I was doing.

Maura McIntyre, a bright light who helped me through the too-many-to-count stuck moments of this project. Her positive, powerful feedback about what I was writing and creating inspired me to keep going and I'm grateful to her for holding my vision when I lost sight of it.

And finally, deep gratitude to my parents, Rachel and George, and to my brother Joe, for their love, affection, wisdom and the Tamari sense of humour, especially in those dark moments.